GROWING UP  CREATIVE

GROWING UP CREATIVE

Nurturing a Lifetime of Creativity

TERESA M. AMABILE, Ph.D.

C.E.F. Press  ®

The Creative Education Foundation ®

Buffalo, N.Y.

To Christene, my Petunia Patch

Published by CEF Press
1050 Union Road Box 4
Buffalo, NY 14224

Manufactured in the United States of America
Library of Congress Cataloging-in-Publication Data
Amabile, Teresa.
      Growing up creative/by Teresa M. Amabile
          p. cm.
      1. Creative thinking (Education)   2. Creative ability in children
I. Title
LB1062.A47   1989
370.157— dc20
ISBN: 0-930222-89-X
(Hard cover previously published by Crown Publishers, Inc., ISBN 0-517-56939-6)
Cover Design: Wendy Caldwell Maloney and Mary Mathilde Conboy
Second Edition 1992, 2nd Printing 1994, 3rd Printing 1996

CONTENTS

PREFACE

Beauty is all about us, but how many are blind to it! They look at the wonder of this earth—and seem to see nothing. Each second we live in a new and unique moment of the universe, a moment that never was before and will never be again. And what do we teach our children in school? We teach them that two and two make four, and that Paris is the capital of France. When will we also teach them what they are?

You should say to each of them: Do you know what you are? You are a marvel. You are unique. In all the world there is no other child exactly like you. In the millions of years that have passed there has never been a child like you. And look at your body—what a wonder it is! Your legs, your arms, your cunning fingers, the way you move! You may become a Shakespeare, a Michelangelo, a Beethoven. You have the capacity for anything. Yes, you are a marvel.

PABLO   CASALS

*A*ll children are marvels. All children can be creative, and they can remain creative as adults. That is the basic philosophy of this book.

Growing up creative is not easy. I know from personal experience that we all must find our own ways to best use our creative energies. As a child I loved science. I studied chemistry in college and, though I graduated with top honors, I felt that something was missing. When the other research assistants and I would go to lunch with the professors, I noticed that our mentors could barely stop talking about their work. They exchanged ideas constantly, laughed about small setbacks or celebrated triumphs, and generally seemed consumed with interest in the subject. When we left the lunch table, it was always strewn with napkins showing hastily sketched diagrams and equations. That's what was missing in me: an all-consuming love of chemistry.

I did feel that kind of love, however, when I began to study psychology and particularly the psychology of creativity. This, too, was science—but a fascinating science of people and how they create. The lesson I learned from my experience is the main point of this book: creativity is impossible without that inner spark.

As long as they have that spark, everyone can be creative. Creativity is not the sole province of "gifted" and "talented" people, although they may have greater potential that can be used in creative ways. Creativity can and should be a part of the daily life of all children and adults.

Traditionally, writing and research on children's creativity have emphasized talent, personality, and the training of special creativity skills. I believe that such an emphasis is misguided. The most crucial factor in creativity is the *motivation* to do something creative. Talent, personality, and skill tell us what a child *can* do; motivation tells us what that child *will* do.

Children's social environment (at home and in school) can have a significant impact on their motivation. Practically speaking, focusing on the motivation to be creative can be much more useful than focusing on talent. It is much easier for parents and teachers to improve the child's home and school environment than to change that child's personality or drastically increase his store of talent.

In this book, you'll learn:

- What children's creativity is, and how you can recognize it
- The basic components of children's creativity and stages of the creative process
- The importance of motivation in creativity
- How home and school environments can destroy children's creativity
- Several specific techniques that parents and teachers can use to keep children's creativity alive

The information and advice in this book comes from several sources:

First, my own thirteen years of research on creativity, as well as the work of dozens of other creativity researchers. My research has consisted of both laboratory experiments on creativity and field observations, with preschool children, elementary school children, college students, creative writers, and other working adults.

Second, in-depth interviews I conducted with the novelist John Irving (author of *The World According to Garp* and several other books), the child-playwright Jason Brown (author of *Tender Places*), and Jason's mother, Carol. In the interview with John Irving, I probed his memory of the environment in which he grew up, and the development of his own motivation for creativity. In the interviews with Jason Brown and his mother, I examined the actual ongoing childhood environment that nurtures this young boy's creativity.

Third, talks I have had with dozens of parents and teachers. Some of these were formal interviews, some were informal discussions, some came during the course of work on my book *Psychological Research in the Classroom*, with Peggy Stubbs, and some occurred during question-and-answer periods after my speeches to parent and teacher groups (where the speaker often learns more than the audience).

Fourth, the autobiographies, biographies, journals, and letters of several famous creative people in a variety of fields.

Fifth, my postcollege experience teaching at St. Louis Elementary School in Pittsford, New York.

Sixth, my own life. My childhood home was highly conducive to creativity. My brother, my five sisters, and I were given a wide range of interesting, challenging experiences by our parents. As a result, our adulthoods show a rather high level of creativity. Among the seven siblings, there is an artist, a high school English teacher, a junior high school French teacher, an advertising copywriter, a psychology professor, an English professor, the director of a hospital's cardiac rehabilitation unit, a lawyer, a doctor, a handicrafts expert, a journalist, two small-business owners, an accomplished cook, and two published writers. (I know that's more than seven professions, but a number of us lead multiple lives.)

Finally, I have learned about children's creativity by living and growing for seven years with my daughter, Christene.

I would like to acknowledge the sources of support that my creativity research has received over the years: the Foundation for Child Development, the National Institute for Child Health and Human Development, the National Institute of Mental Health, a series of Biomedical Research Support Grants from the National Institutes of Health, and the Mazer Family Fund at Brandeis University.

A number of elementary schools in the Boston area graciously allowed my students and me to conduct our research with their children and teachers, and I would like to thank them, too: St. Jude School, St. Clement School, St. Agnes School, St. John's School, St. Anthony's School, the Amesbury Public Schools, and the Lemberg Children's Center at Brandeis University.

I would like to thank the outstanding individuals who gave so much time to let me interview them: John Irving, Jason Brown, Carol Brown-Cohen, and teacher Laura Kesten. I am also deeply indebted to people who, as students, research assistants, and friends, have collaborated on my creativity research over the years: Beth Hennessey, Karl Hill, Peggy Stubbs, Barbara S. Grossman, Judy Gitomer, Carolyn Amabile Ross, and Phyllis Amabile. A number of friends and colleagues helped me by providing insightful comments on this manuscript, and I deeply appreciate their assistance, as well: Bronwen Cheek, Nancy Fulmines, Mary Amabile Gosch, Tina Green, Beth Hennessey, Laura Kesten, Peggy Stubbs, and Mick Watson. Barbara Grossman of Crown Publishers nurtured my creativity with sound advice and ample encouragement. Rona Leff did a wonderful job helping me prepare the manuscript.

Finally, I wish to thank my richest source of inspiration, Christene Amabile DeJong.

1

VISION AND PASSION

Get a clear, consistent vision of your child as an adult, and make sure the vision fits your child's unique individuality.

True creativity is impossible without some measure of passion.

THE VISIONS THAT WE PRESENT TO OUR
CHILDREN SHAPE THE FUTURE. THEY BECOME
SELF-FULFILLING PROPHECIES. DREAMS ARE
MAPS.

Carl Sagan

*I*magine that it is a warm spring evening twenty years
from now. You sit in your living room, listening to
music, thinking about your children. You smile with
relief at the realization that they have made it safely into
adulthood. You think back on their growing-up years, glanc-
ing at the childhood photographs on the mantel. Then, to
feed both your memory and your pride, you walk to the
bookshelf and take down their college yearbooks. You open
to the appropriate pages and find your grown children smiling out at you.

Can you see them? Can you picture these adult children
of yours? Try to visualize the shape of your daughter's face,
the tilt of her head, the size of her hands. Try to imagine
how tall your son will be, or what shape his mouth will have.
Try to see your grown-up children looking at you, talking,
laughing; try to project your college yearbook photographs
onto your mental screen.

I have often tried this exercise with the face of my
daughter, who is now seven—and I have always failed. The
image goes in and out of focus, changing with the play of
possibilities across it. Most people have trouble forming a
picture of what a child will look like as an adult—even if that
child is their own. And yet, when we look at the baby pictures
of adults that we know, the resemblance is usually so close as

to be laughable. *Of course* this is what that baby face should have grown into! But we can't do the same in reverse. We can't develop a clear future picture of any child with that same sense of certainty.

Now try to imagine what kind of people your children will grow into. What is printed in those yearbooks about personality, hobbies, activities? What fields of study have your children chosen? Have they done anything creative in writing, art, business, science, drama?

You'll probably find this exercise a bit easier than imagining your child's grown face. You may already have drawn some conclusions about your son's adult personality from the way he hides in his room with his gerbils and science books or charms the neighbors into buying candy from his Boy Scout troop. You may have some information about your future daughter from having watched her take out the paint box every day after school or challenge her classmates to footraces. By watching carefully, you can develop a clear image of what your child will be—in terms of personality, values, attitudes, interests, accomplishments.

This is your *vision* for your child—the image you have of where that child is going, what that child will be. You may think that it doesn't matter very much what you imagine for your son or daughter, that they will turn out in some predetermined way regardless of what vision you have in your mind. But it does matter, a great deal. Your vision can shape how happy, productive, and creative your child will be.

Why should you care about your child's creativity? Because all of human progress requires adult creativity, and people are more likely to do creative work as adults if they develop the skill and the motivation for creativity as children.

But there are other good reasons to care about creativity in children. One of my favorite cartoons shows a wizened old man with his finger raised. The caption: " 'It was hell,' recalls former child." Childhood isn't easy. Creativity can make it more fun and easier to cope with. Contrary to some popular views, doing creative work does not mean living a neurotic, unhappy life. Highly creative people tend to be quite strong and flexible emotionally. In fact, some psychologists say that creativity and psychological health go hand in hand.

VISION:
THE PABLO CASALS STORY

You may have heard the word *vision* from successful corporate executives. Researchers who have looked for differences between creative corporations and stagnant ones have found a consistent pattern: The creative winners are headed by leaders who have a clear vision for their corporation, a vision that goes beyond next quarter's earnings or this month's production schedule. These leaders have a vision of where the organization is going, what it will be in five or ten years, and what it will have accomplished. Their visions are bold and optimistic, and are clearly communicated to every single member of the organization.

You, as parent and as teacher, are a leader. Probably more than any single thing you will do or say to your children, the vision you have for each of them will be crucial in the development of their motivation, creativity, and ultimate achievement. You communicate that vision in what you say about them and their future, in your reactions to their achievements large and small, in your approval or disapproval of choices they make, and even in your comments about children, adults, and life in general.

What kind of parental vision can inspire your children to creative achievement, give them confidence and self-esteem, lead them to develop a firm guiding vision of their own lives?

First, your vision should be clear with respect to basic life principles. You, yourself, should have a firm notion of the values, standards, and principles you would like your children to follow throughout life.

Second, your vision for each child should be shaped by the temperament, personality, needs, and interests of that particular child. It does no good (and a great deal of harm) to develop a vision of your son as a physician if his interests lie in the arts rather than the sciences, and if he would rather work by himself than with others. Pushing children into activities that do not fit them as individuals can cause them a great deal of anger and frustration and can lead to a sorry waste of their real talents. This is perhaps the simplest and most straightforward principle of child guidance, yet a disturbingly large number of people seem unaware of it.

Third, whatever the other specifics of your vision, you should imagine your adult children as independent and passionately interested in whatever work they choose. Of all the characteristics of well-known creative people, independence and passion are the ones that appear most consistently across different fields and through different generations.

The story of Pablo Casals, the world-renowned cellist, composer, and conductor, gives us an inspiring example of parental vision. Pablo's mother, Pilar, though not a musician herself, recognized in her son both a high level of musical talent and a great interest in all aspects of music. While Pablo's father failed to envision any future for his son in music (though he was a musician himself), Pablo's mother developed a firm and clear vision of the contribution her son might make to the world through his music. That vision helped Pablo develop one of his own, one that carried him through an astonishingly successful career of more than eighty years. In his autobiography, he says:

> It was a truly remarkable thing. My mother
> had had some musical training, but she was
> not of course a musician in the sense my
> father was. Yet she knew what my future
> was to be. She knew; and she always acted

on the knowledge with a firmness and certainty and calmness that has never ceased to
amaze me.

This mother's vision was built on a keen understanding
of her child's special qualities. After hearing a cello for the
first time, Pablo was filled with a fervor to learn the instrument. Pablo's father was not moved by his son's pleas, but his
mother's reaction was quite different:

> My mother understood what had happened.
> She told my father, "Pablo shows such en-
> thusiasm for the cello that he must have the
> chance really to study it. There is no teacher
> here in Vendrell who is qualified to teach
> him properly. We must arrange for him to
> go to the School of Music in Barcelona."

Casals describes the impact of his mother's vision:

> If it had not been for my mother's convic-
> tion and determination that music was my
> destiny, it is quite conceivable that I would
> have become a carpenter.

Notice two important features of Pilar Casals's vision for
her young Pablo. First, it was quite clear. She saw her son as
a musician, as someone whose life focused on giving great
music to the world. Second, that well-defined vision did not
develop from some fantasy the mother had, some wish that
had nothing to do with reality. Rather, it developed from her
close and loving observation of her son as an individual with
his own particular skills and interests.

Pablo Casals was, of course, quite precocious, in both the
development of his skill and the development of his interest.

Few very young children display such definite passion for a given pursuit. And *passion* is the word for it:

> Music was inside me and all about me; it was the air I breathed from the time I could walk. To hear my father play the piano was an ecstasy for me. When I was two or three, I would sit on the floor beside him as he played, and I would press my head against the piano in order to absorb the sound more completely.

This early rapture with music would develop into a specific passion for the cello while Pablo was still a boy:

> When I was eleven years old, I heard the cello played for the first time. From the moment I heard the first notes, I was overwhelmed. I felt as if I could not breathe. There was something so tender, beautiful, and human—yes, so very human—about the sound. I had never heard such a beautiful sound before. A radiance filled me. When the first composition was ended, I told my father, "Father, that is the most wonderful instrument I have ever heard. That is what I want to play."

This kind of passionate interest is the hallmark of true adult creativity. It is described again and again by researchers who have worked with outstandingly creative people. It is what leads some people to do creative work even when they are living in dire circumstances. People sometimes think such incidents mean that suffering contributes to creativity, that insecurity, hunger, and cold somehow strengthen the soul or sharpen the senses. Not at all. Researchers have no evidence that genius will flourish under conditions of physical deprivation. But we do have evidence that extremely creative people are *possessed;* they are possessed with a constant desire to do their work, to say something through it, to leave some lasting contribution. If a starving artist does a series of masterpieces, it is not because of the starvation, but in spite of it.

PASSION FOR LEARNING: THE ISAAC ASIMOV STORY

If they will one day be creative, must all children show the kind of passion demonstrated by young Pablo Casals— sharp, burning, and focused on a specific field? No. Most creative work in the world is done by people who did not show such extraordinary passion as children. But children can learn to develop that kind of focused interest in doing something for its own sake—because it is intriguing, involving, challenging. Often this kind of passion begins to show up in children as a love of learning. All children are born curious.

Consider the childhood of Isaac Asimov, the famous writer of science and science fiction who now has nearly three hundred books to his credit. Because his family emigrated to the United States when he was three, he had to pick up English on his own, through daily life in Brooklyn. This kind of situation is not terribly unusual. But young Isaac was so strongly curious about everything around him that he soon began to puzzle over newspapers, street signs, and anything else that had words on it. For months, he hounded his older playmates into teaching him the alphabet, demonstrating the sounds that letters made, and telling him if he was correct as he tried to sound out words. He was so consumed with curiosity that he even figured out the role of silent letters. (He and his mother were on a train to Coney

Island, and he soon realized, by listening to people chatting about their destination, that the *s* in that strange second word was not supposed to be pronounced.)

So it was that Isaac Asimov learned to read before the age of five, even though his father could not read English, his mother could not speak English, he had no older siblings, and he had not yet started school. Within a year, he had gotten his first library card and was withdrawing as many books as he was allowed, as frequently as he was allowed.

Obviously, Asimov was different from Casals in terms of how specific his childhood interests were. Casals was playing the cello quite well by the age of twelve. Asimov was not writing science fiction quite well (or at all) by the age of twelve. But, much earlier than that, he *was* beginning to show a passion of one type—the love of learning, which all children share. It is this that gives parents and teachers the most promising foundation for building in their children a lifelong passion for learning and creating.

ORDINARY CHILDREN
CAN DO EXTRAORDINARY THINGS:
THE JASON HARDMAN STORY

You may believe that your child has some very special talents, but you may also see a considerable gap between the formidable talents of Casals or Asimov and the skill that your child displays. Certainly, if either of these geniuses were to appear as a student in a good American school system of today, he would be identified as unusually gifted. Most children, perhaps yours included, are not identified as extremely gifted at an early age. But this *doesn't* mean that your child cannot do extremely creative work as an adult. Most creative work is done by people who were not called geniuses as children. We would be making a terrible mistake if we focused all our hopes for creativity on the few young prodigies of the world.

Even people who actually do creative work as children often seem quite ordinary in many respects. Jason Hardman was ten years old in 1980 and seemed much like any other bright, interesting boy when he moved with his family to Elsinore, a tiny town in Utah. There was only one thing about Elsinore that Jason really disliked: the nearest library was in a town six miles away, and they would only let him borrow three books a week. So, simply to feed his own interest and enjoyment in reading, this ordinary boy did an extraordinarily creative thing: he started his own public library.

Jason began by investigating the storeroom that held books from Elsinore's last public library (which had been closed for several years due to lack of funds). With his parents' encouragement, he appeared before the town council and asked their permission to use the books and an unfinished room in the town hall basement. He then phoned the mayor daily to ask for a decision. Once permission was granted, he enlisted the help of volunteers to clean the room, wire it for electricity, and build bookshelves. Jason collected books from anyone he could convince to make a donation. And then, just as he had dreamed, Jason opened his library with the four thousand books he had gathered and his homemade cataloging system. He ran the whole operation after school every afternoon.

Before long, people all over the country were reading newspaper and magazine articles about Jason's achievement. He was asked to testify at a congressional hearing about the needs of rural libraries in America. He appeared on "The Tonight Show" and "Good Morning America," received a full scholarship to the University of Southern California, addressed the Utah State Legislature, and, finally, was given an award in the White House by President Ronald Reagan.

Yet none of that had been part of Jason's original vision.

He was not labeled as a genius in school, and he had not previously shown any particular talents for leadership or creative achievement. He simply had a strong interest in reading and a dream. He also had parents who knew how to recognize his interest, nurture his dream, and provide him with an environment where his creativity could blossom.

SHAPING THE VISION

The first step for you to take in developing a vision for your child is to find out what the child's own vision is for the future. Here is an exercise designed to help you. It is most appropriate for children over the age of six or so, although you can adapt it for younger children. Ask your child to answer these questions, or answer them as you think your child would.

FUTURE PERFECT

1. I am thirty years old, and I've been out of college for eight years. It's the year _____.

2. My occupation is:

3. I live in:

4. The things I like to do best are:

5. At work, I'm really good at:

6. At home, I'm really good at:

7. Here's what I like most about my life:

8. This is the kind of thirty-year-old person I am:

9. The most important thing I learned from my parents was:

10. The thing I like best about myself is:

Now have a go at writing out your vision for your child. The following exercise will help you put together the elements of your vision:

YOUR VISION FOR YOUR CHILD

1. How has this child surprised you?

2. In what ways is this child different from your other children, or other children you know?

3. List the things this child most enjoys doing.

4. List the things this child is best at.

5. In what activities does this child currently show creativity?

6. In what fields and areas of adult life do you think this child might show creativity?

7. List the major values, standards, and principles you would like your child to follow throughout life.

8. What is your vision of this child as an adult? List everything you consider important.

As we look deeper into the issues of children's creativity and how it can be nurtured, try to keep your vision firmly in mind. And remember: No matter what you give your child in terms of education, skill development, materials, instruments, or interesting experiences, you are missing out on the most important element if you do not help your child develop a deep sense of interest and excitement about learning. Without that sense, your child could end up as one of those promising, talented, advantaged people who somehow drift through life with their promise unfulfilled. But *with* that sense, your child has a good chance of developing the kind of passion that can carry a person through rigorous training, repeated failure, financial struggle—even a little starvation —to the glory of full-blown adult creativity.

2

RECOGNIZING CHILDREN'S CREATIVITY

Creativity is not the same thing as intelligence or eccentricity.

A child's behavior is creative if it is novel and appropriate.

Any normal human being is capable of producing creative work in some area, at some time.

me and
cassie

*M*ichelle and Emily, both four years old, are discussing how to spend their Saturday afternoon. "Let's play house, with two moms and six kids."

"Naw, we did that before lunch."

"I know! Let's play my dad's new game—Trivial Pursuit!"

"We can't play that; it's just for grown-ups."

"How do you know?"

"Because it's called Trivial Pursuit. Trivial *means* grown-up!"

To the adult overhearing this conversation, the conclusion that trivial means grown-up seemed particularly amusing, apt, and even insightful. But was it creative? Everyone has heard remarks from children that are surprising and impressive in some way. Each of us has seen children do things that are unusual, well-executed, or particularly lovely. Each of us has seen offbeat, nonconforming, undisciplined behavior from children. How can we decide if the things a child says and does are truly creative? If we want to promote creativity in children, what is it we are promoting?

Consider these brief scenes. Are they similar to things your own children have done? Would you say they are examples of creativity?

• Michael is twelve and has had his personal computer for three years. He spends long hours alone in his room, playing with different programming techniques and reading computer publications. Last year, his parents purchased a modem so that Michael could get an account on the computer system that serves his junior high school. Michael figures out how to tap into the grading records and changes transcripts for himself and his friends.

• Madeline's fifth-grade class is given an assignment to "write a 750-word essay on China." She turns in a 750-word story about her summer vacation, which she wrote in marking pen on several pieces of china that she bought at a flea market.

• Four-year-old Christene and her mother are waiting for their dinner at a restaurant. Using the pad and pen they brought along, Christene draws an elaborate puzzle for her mother to solve. (See Figure 1.) After her mother has made several attempts at providing solutions, Christene explains: "The answer to the puzzle is *me!* These lines stand for my wavy hair, the numbers show that I'm four going on five, and the rest doesn't stand for anything at all!"

• Jonathan comes home from the second grade on a rainy afternoon, sits at the kitchen table with his crayons, and makes a drawing entitled "Rainbow." It depicts several clouds with bow ties falling from them.

• Alyson's kindergarten class is learning about dinosaurs. She brings home the brontosaurus picture she colored; the animal is striped, like a zebra, in fifteen different colors. (See Figure 2.) When asked about it, she says, "The teacher said to color it any way we wanted!"

• Though clearly not malicious toward others, eleven-year-old Todd is decidedly "different." Whatever all the other children are doing, whatever teachers and parents re-

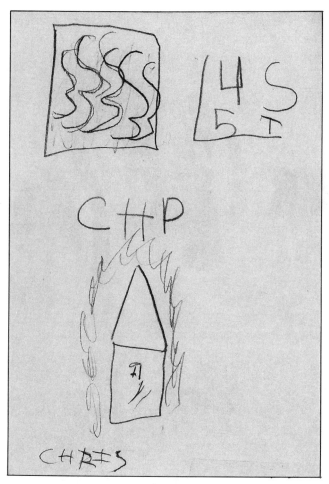

Figure 1

quest, he does something else. In general, he rejects anything that is conventional or authoritarian.

• Before setting off for the fourth grade every morning, Katy ties a colorful rag around a clump of her hair, pulls her T-shirt down so that it hangs out from under her sweatshirt, and removes the laces from her tennis shoes.

• Andrew, who is just learning to read and write, draws two fish and then neatly labels the drawing. (See Figure 3.)

Figure 2

Figure 3

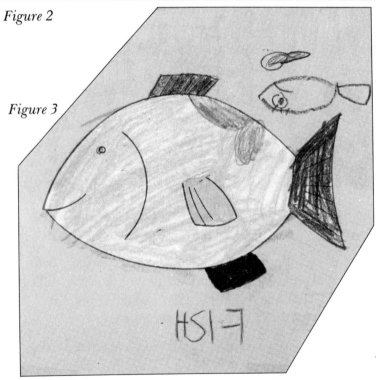

Fearing dyslexia, and never having noticed that Andrew printed backward before, his father asks why the word is printed that way. Andrew replies, matter-of-fact, "Well, the fish are *swimming* that way [right to left]!"

• Three-year-old Jennifer has, after many hours of playing with her shoes, figured out how to tie the laces in nice, tight bows. No adult has ever tried to teach her this skill. After several weeks of watching Jennifer and practicing on her own, Jennifer's twin sister, Julie, also manages to tie her shoes.

• Eleven-year-old Seth is known as the Numbers Wizard in his midwestern community. He can mentally multiply any two two-digit numbers as fast as any hand calculator. So far, he has never made a mistake.

Which of these children is showing creativity? What *is* creativity? And what isn't it?

WHAT CREATIVITY ISN'T

Most of us think of creativity in terms of *the person*. We tend to believe that creativity is something that exists in a person; we say things like, "This child is very creative."

Often, people mistakenly use the word *creative* as a synonym for *gifted*. They mean that the child has unusual talent in some area, or that the child is highly intelligent. A child who masters a musical instrument at a young age is indeed gifted, and so is a child who scores unusually high on an IQ test.

But creativity is not the same as talent or intelligence. In the 1920s, thousands of California schoolchildren were tested, and several hundred of them were identified as "gifted." The children's progress was followed with tests and questionnaires throughout their adult lives. As of the 1970s, however, not one of the "gifted" children had become well-known for creativity in some field. Moreover, creativity researchers have discovered that both high and low levels of creativity can be found in highly intelligent children—*and* in children of average intelligence.

This means that, unless he has devised some new mathematical system, Seth, the Numbers Wizard, is probably not showing a very high level of creativity. Most likely, he has memorized the multiplication table up to 99 times 99, and has practiced them well enough to be able to recite them almost automatically. Of course, this sort of performance requires a great deal of intelligence. High intelligence, yes. High creativity, no.

Another characteristic that is often mistaken as a sign of creativity is eccentricity. People who behave strangely, who refuse to conform to society, who consistently act like misfits, even people who seem mentally unbalanced in some way, may be called creative—especially by those of us inclined toward kindness. But does strangeness imply creativity? The answer is complicated, because we can all easily point to examples of famous creative people who were mentally unbalanced, or even insane: Vincent van Gogh, who cut off his own ear and later committed suicide; Edgar Allen Poe, who was severely depressed and an alcoholic; the poet Ezra Pound, who was diagnosed as schizophrenic.

To date, the best evidence that we have suggests nothing more than a slight relationship between some types of creativity and mental disorder. It's true, for example, that compared to the general population, creative writers show a slightly higher incidence of depression. But this evidence by no means suggests that strange, eccentric, or unbalanced behavior is necessary for or helpful to creativity. Many psychologists believe just the opposite: that people can best display their creativity when they are free of anxieties and mental disorders. Extremely creative people tend to be un-conforming—that *is* true—but they also tend to be strong mentally and emotionally. Young Todd, who rejects author-ity and adopts nonconformist behaviors simply to be differ-ent, is not necessarily creative. Being different for its own sake, as a goal in itself, is not sufficient for creativity.

So creativity is not the same thing as intelligence or gift-edness, and it is not the same thing as eccentricity. Creativity is also not sheer imitation or memorization; it is not mere accident, where the child makes a mistake without realizing there is some meaning or value in the mistake; and it is not bizarre, erratic, or uncontrolled thinking.

The three-year-old twin Julie, who learned to tie her shoes by imitating her sister, Jennifer, is not showing creativ-ity. She *is* showing learning, and very impressive learning for a three-year-old, at that. Jennifer's behavior, on the other hand, is quite an extreme example of creativity. She has never been shown how to tie shoelaces; she simply played around with her own laces, trying new combinations and learning from trial and error, until she hit upon a workable method.

Obviously, experience and context have to figure into our assessment of creativity, too. If Katy is really the first to dress with colorful rags in her hair, a hanging-out T-shirt, and laceless sneakers, then her behavior can be considered creative. But if, like so many other girls her age, she has seen singers, movie stars, models, or her classmates dress in this way, her behavior should be considered the height of imita-tion and conformity—no matter how offbeat it might appear to bewildered adults.

What about happy accidents, those mistakes children make that lead us to wish *we* had thought of something so clever? Are they being creative, or merely ignorant? Again, it depends. If Michelle and Emily realized that they were making a wry comment on adult society when they said that trivial meant grown-up, then they were showing verbal creativity far beyond their years. But they probably had no idea what the word *trivial* really means. Most likely, their parents had told them that Trivial Pursuit was a grown-up game, so they equated the name of the game with its audience.

And little Andrew, writing *fish* backward, probably had no inkling that writing the word in the direction of the swimming fish was a clever thing to do. The idea might legitimately be considered creative—if it were done deliberately. But Andrew simply didn't know the written language well enough to realize that he was doing something out of the ordinary.

Certainly, unintentional mistakes can lead to great creativity. The history of science is full of such stories. Alexander Fleming was probably not the first scientist to leave a bacteria culture accidentally exposed to air so that a mold grew and killed the bacteria. But Fleming realized that there could be important uses for a mold that kills bacteria. And his recognition of the significance of this accident led to the development of penicillin.

There is a similar story about the development of Scotchgard, the spray-on-protector of upholstery and other fabrics. A 3M scientist, working with the new fluorochemicals the company was developing, accidentally let some drip onto his tennis shoes. We can assume that he was not the only scientist to have unintentionally splashed some of the substance onto fabric. But he *was* the only one to recognize the importance of the fact that this spot did not get soiled along with the rest of the sneaker.

So mistakes *can* be important elements of the creative process. But a child's mistake, even if it appears clever or appropriate to an observer, cannot be considered creative unless the child recognizes its significance or actually intended to do something different.

WHAT CREATIVITY IS

Anything that a child does or says can be considered creative if it meets two criteria. First, it must be substantially different from anything the child has done before and anything the child has seen or heard before. Second, it cannot be *merely* different; it should be correct, useful toward achieving a goal, appealing, or meaningful to the child in some way. Most psychologists who study creativity label these criteria *novelty* and *appropriateness*.

The novelty criterion is fairly straightforward. The child's behavior cannot be just an imitation or recitation of something he or she has seen before; *within the child's repertoire of behavior,* it must be novel in some significant way. To make a judgment about novelty, we need to know something about the child's previous knowledge and experience.

The criterion of appropriateness is more troublesome. We use it in order to rule out behaviors that are merely bizarre, but it is a slippery concept. If we are talking about mathematics or science or grammar, then something is appropriate if it is *correct.* But what about art, music, storytelling, fantasy play? How can we speak of appropriateness there? Ultimately, it is in the eye of the beholder. If a child's novel behavior is somehow pleasing or communicative or meaningful—at least to the child, in our estimation—then we can say that it is appropriate.

The appropriateness criterion rules out behaviors that are novel but somehow wrong, such as mistaking the word *trivial* for *grown-up* or failing to realize that the word *fish* was printed backward. Still, we can consider other of our examples as truly creative. Christene's puzzle had at least a spark of creativity in it. True, she wasn't following the usual rules of puzzle-making (the puzzle should be solvable by other people!), but her drawings of herself *were* both novel and appropriate. She does, indeed, have wavy hair (as shown by the wavy lines she drew). And she was, in fact, four going on five.

Jonathan and Alyson also showed creativity in their rainbow and dinosaur drawings. Jonathan had never seen a picture of bow ties falling from the sky, so the drawing was certainly novel for him (and perhaps it was novel compared to all children's drawings). In addition to being novel, his visual pun for the ordinary word *rainbow* is charmingly appropriate. Similarly, Alyson did appropriately fulfill the requirements of her assignment to color in the brontosaurus outline, but she took full advantage of the freedom to do it in any way she wanted. As a result, her creation was truly novel *and* appropriate—in other words, creative.

But is it creative when a child quite knowingly bends the rules by assuming (or taking) more freedom than exists in a situation, or when a child actually breaks the rules? Take Madeline, who used the word *china* as a pun to escape from having to actually write a report on China. Or Michael, who used his knowledge of computers to create a program that quite illegally changed school grades. Was their behavior novel? Decidedly. It is doubtful that any other child has ever turned in a school assignment written on old pieces of china, as Madeline did. And Michael clearly created his own program for electronic breaking and entering. Was their behavior appropriate? Again, the concept is a slippery one. It was not ethically appropriate. But it *was* meaningful and purposeful to the children. Because of this, we should probably consider their behavior creative—though we may do so reluctantly.

Taken strictly, the definition of creativity as "novel and appropriate behavior" is value-free—if we take "appropriate" to mean technically correct or useful. Destructive, illegal, immoral behaviors can be just as creative as constructive and positive ones. This may be difficult to accept because, in general usage, the word *creative* has a very positive connotation. But much can be learned from considering even hideously antisocial behaviors creative, if they are novel and appropriate in achieving a goal.

The *process* of creative thinking—the process of coming up with something creative—is essentially the same regardless of the results. When people are successfully coming up with new ways to do things, new ways to think about things, new ways to make things, they are thinking and acting in the same ways regardless of whether they are inventing a cancer treatment or a nerve gas. What becomes important is that we teach our children not only the skills they need to be creative, but the values they need to use that creativity in a positive way.

A FIELD GUIDE TO RECOGNIZING CREATIVITY IN CHILDREN

If someone asked you to give an honest assessment of how smart your child is, you might think of mentioning the score your child achieved on some objective test—an achievement test, a national scholarship test, an entrance examination, an IQ test. And if someone asked you to give an honest assessment of how creative your child is, you might want to have a score on some objective test of creativity. In fact, there are such tests, and many children have taken them in school.

The creativity tests given in schools usually contain these types of questions: How many uses can you think of for a brick (or a paper clip, or some other common object)? How can this toy be improved? What can you draw from this squiggle? What sort of ending can you think up for this story? What would happen if we woke up tomorrow and everyone was ten inches high? Children's answers to these questions are scored according to four general criteria: (1) the sheer number of answers the child gives to a question (the more the better); (2) the number of different types of answers the child gives (such as different *types* of uses for a brick—using it to weigh things down, using it to build things, etc.); (3) the *unusualness* of the child's answers, considering the answers given by other children; and (4) how much the child elaborates on each answer (the amount of detail in what the child puts down).

Without a doubt, these tests do measure some mental abilities that are related to creativity. But many other abilities, as well as motivation, play a crucial role in creative thinking, and these are not tapped by creativity tests. So if your child receives high scores on these tests, you can be encouraged that some of the skills for creativity are already in place. But if your child does not do well on these tests, there is no cause for despair. Such skills can always be developed.

Creativity tests have other drawbacks. They are often administered in testlike situations at school, where children are likely to be anxious and inflexible in their thinking. In a school setting, children might start to believe that there are "right" and "wrong" answers—which, in fact, there *are* on some of these tests! If we define creative answers as being *novel*, it doesn't make much sense to look only for certain types of answers. And it doesn't seem right to look at the *number* of answers as a measure of creativity. Finally, and most important, scores on these tests can be used to *label* a child as creative or uncreative. Social psychologists have known for decades that labeling can create biases and can lead the labeled person to live up to the label in unconscious ways.

Parents and teachers would be much better off if they used their own careful observation of children in order to identify creativity, and viewed tests as merely supplementary information. In fact, intelligent observation is superior to testing in two important ways.

First, observation focuses on the child's behavior rather than on the child as an object to be tested. This helps to avoid the problem of labeling. Instead of saying, "Sue is very creative," a teacher can make much more useful statements such as, "Sue's artwork is very creative when she's allowed to choose her own project within loose guidelines," or "Sue's writing of poetry seems to be much more creative than her writing of stories." And, instead of saying, "Jeremy is not a creative kid," a parent can say, "Jeremy seems to be afraid of trying something new when playing games with the family, but does show some creativity in inventing games with his friends."

The second advantage of observation is that it will probably be more accurate. As I said earlier, creativity tests are too narrow. Careful observation is likely to reveal a greater range of the abilities and motivations that feed into creativity. Moreover, a greater knowledge of how a child acts will allow us to say whether a behavior is really novel for that child. Remember the shoe-tying twins. Most likely, only the twins' parents would be able to appreciate Jennifer's creativity, because only they would know that she had never been taught how to tie shoes. You can be sure that no test score would have picked that up!

How can you make a reasonable assessment of your child's creativity? The most important first step is to develop a vigilance for creativity, a mind-set in which you have creativity on your mental agenda whenever you are with the child. Also keep in mind that judging creativity in children isn't always easy. How do you really know if something your son does is truly new for him? How can you tell if the clever thing your daughter just said really means anything to her? Is true creativity developing here, or was it just an accident?

But don't worry. If you watch your child carefully, and you *think* you see real creativity, you probably do. As a friend of mine put it, "When in doubt, I assume that if *my* kid did it, it must be creative!" What harm can it do?

Of course, children at different ages show very different types of creative behaviors. The areas in which children display creativity, and the levels of creativity they show, depend on their education, their experience, and their level of both cognitive and physical development. Here is a simple guide to the kind of creativity you might see in children of various ages:

TABLE 1

Age*	Area	Examples of Creative Behavior
2–3	Singing	Rather than simply repeating songs they have heard, inventing melodies or putting their own nonsense words to familiar songs.
	Drawing	Playing around with different lines, shapes, and colors.
	Building	Experimenting with various types of structures.
	Playing Instruments	Trying out combinations of sounds on toy instruments or household objects.
4–5	Painting	Combining colors in new ways, using both brushes and fingers.
	Word Play	Playing with the sounds and meanings of words, often while talking to themselves.
	Dancing	Using dance as a way of expressing feeling or experimenting with physical motion.

* Age ranges are approximate averages. Children at each age also show more advanced versions of the creative behaviors typical of the younger ages, and less developed versions of the creative behaviors typical of older ages.

4–5	Fantasy	Inventing imaginary playmates or assuming the role of pretend characters playing out pretend events.
6–7	Cooking	Experimenting, under adult supervision, with food combinations; using food as an art form.
	Sculpture	Using clay, sand, and other materials to make various shapes.
	Drama	Making up and acting out plays, including costumes, songs, and dialogue.
	Social Relations	Adopting new and useful solutions to interpersonal conflicts.
8–9	Storytelling	Sustaining a coherent storyline with invented characters and situations.
	Games	Inventing elaborate games with rules and goals.
	Dressing	Deliberately putting together outfits that combine clothing styles in unusual ways.
10–11	Numbers	Playing with ways of using numbers to describe things.
	Language	Creating secret words or languages with siblings or small groups of friends. (This can occur earlier in twins.)

10–11	Visual World	Decorating living environments, often in idiosyncratic ways around themes that hold personal meaning.
12–13	Machines	Studying mechanical and electronic devices, often rebuilding them or using them in new ways.
	Information	Gathering information in logical ways, experimenting, and using inductive and deductive reasoning.
	Writing	Expressing ideas using metaphor and simile, in prose and in poetry.

ORDINARY AND EXTRAORDINARY CREATIVITY

When we hear the phrase "creative person," we are likely to think of someone extraordinary, and probably famous—someone who has led an unconventional life and, in the process, has produced a number of astonishingly creative works. Unfortunately, this implies that very few of us are "creative people," and very few of our children are likely to become so. This is terribly misleading. It suggests that creativity is some permanent part of a person, touching everything that person does, setting that person apart from the rest of the human race. Creativity does *not* describe a person; it describes ideas, behaviors, and products that are appropriately novel. Any normal human being is capable of producing creative work in some area, at some time.

If it's difficult for you to think of your child as truly creative—that six-month-old drooling on her teething ring, or that teenager with the tape player plugged into his ears—

maybe it will help to think of some ordinary children who ended up showing a startling degree of creativity. Recall Jason Hardman, the ten-year-old boy who started a public library using his own ingenuity, imagination, and energy. Here's another story.

A 1984 magazine article described Trevor Ferrell as a "garden variety eleven-year-old," who "plays Pac-Man, enjoys 'Diff'rent Strokes,' and would like to meet Ricky Schroder and Ronald Reagan." But one evening Trevor saw a TV news segment on the plight of the homeless in nearby Philadelphia. Not only was he emotionally moved by what he saw, but he was also moved to imagine possibilities for helping the homeless.

The first night he convinced his parents to drive him into town from their wealthy suburb. He brought an extra pillow and blanket from home and gave them to a man he saw sleeping on a subway vent. The next night he returned with one of his mother's cast-off coats. He came back again and again, with cups of coffee, bags of sandwiches, and armloads of his family's extra clothes. Before too long, he had exhausted his own resources. So Trevor found ways of persuading his community to help out. He handed out flyers, spoke to newspaper reporters, and appealed to his parish church. Eventually, Trevor's "mission" received carloads of donated clothing, baskets of food, large sums of cash, a Volkswagen van, and a thirty-room house in Philadelphia. He has a large and devoted following of street people who depend on him for physical nurturance and emotional comfort.

Certainly, the accomplishments of this "garden variety" child are extraordinary. But are they creative? First, were his actions novel? Decidedly so. Not only were they different from anything that he personally had done before, but they were quite unique among children, and they were even rather unusual among adults. Were they appropriate? Yes.

They were directed toward a particular goal—relieving the suffering of a city's homeless—and they achieved that goal. Moreover, what Trevor did was meaningful not only to him but to others. His accomplishments were truly creative.

3

THE INGREDIENTS OF CREATIVITY

A child's creativity in any domain will depend on three things: (1) skill in the domain, (2) creative working and thinking skills, and (3) intrinsic motivation.

Some elements of creativity are inborn; some depend on learning and experience; and some depend on social environment.

*M*argaret's favorite subject in sixth grade is American History. She finished reading her textbook in the first week of class and has been pestering her teacher and parents for supplementary books ever since. Reading history is the reward she reserves for herself at the end of the evening, when the rest of her homework is done. Although Margaret's memory for dates is very good, she thinks of a history book not as a chronology but as a series of short stories about interesting people from the past. Where the details about those people are not given, she looks them up in the library or imagines them—what they looked like, what they wore, how they spoke, what they felt, what motivated them, how they behaved in public and in their private lives. More than anything else, Margaret loves to imagine these famous historical figures in modern-day America. Would this person be pleased with the way we live under the laws he wrote? Would that person be shocked by the way we speak? Would this one rather live in our century than in hers?

It's difficult to say exactly where Margaret developed this passion for history. She's always been naturally curious about people, watching, listening, asking questions. Her father studied history in college, and the bedtime stories he read—even when Margaret was very young—most often were tales about the early American patriots, the Native Americans, and the founding of the United States. Margaret was enthralled with these stories, more so than her brothers were, and she was quite pleased that she could remember so many of the details. Eventually, she learned to read the stories for herself. And she will never forget the trip her family made to Plimoth Plantation near Plymouth, Massachusetts, when she was six; she was enchanted by the re-created Pilgrim Village and charmed by the employees who adopted the identities of the original settlers.

So Margaret is eager as she waits for the teacher to give out the next history project assignments. These projects are *fun*, as far as she's concerned; she gets to learn about something on her own and then figure out some interesting way to present the information to her classmates. Her teacher talks about these projects as teaching assignments. Each member of the class is given a different topic in a new area of study. They have two weeks to research the topic on their own, using the library and the teacher as resources. Then, over the next two weeks, each student is given fifteen minutes to teach the class what he or she learned, using any method of presentation style that they wish. Most of the students enjoy these segments of the course, although many are apprehensive about preparing on their own and then making a public presentation. Margaret's only fear is that the topic won't be important or challenging enough.

She smiles when she opens her assignment envelope. It simply says The Declaration of Independence. Margaret knows that this is a much broader and more important topic than her last one (Life on the Mayflower), and she is pleased. She knows that meeting *this* challenge will give her a real sense of satisfaction.

Almost immediately, Margaret starts coming up with ideas: she could have a big chart showing the main points in the Declaration of Independence, or she could put the names of the people who wrote the Declaration on the board, . . . but, just as quickly, Margaret stops. She realizes that she's not certain who did the actual writing, and she isn't clear on what the main points were. She goes off to the library—but not just to get the assignment over with. Instead, she sees her trip to the library as a chance to get the raw material for playing this great game.

After a few hours at the library, Margaret has amassed a great stockpile of information. She has made a photocopy of the Declaration itself, looked through a book for young people explaining the language and meaning of each section of the Declaration, written out the dates of important events leading up to and following the Declaration, and read several entries on the Declaration in encyclopedias. Already she has four pages of notes.

Margaret writes down her first two ideas for the presentation. But she's not entirely satisfied with them and pushes herself to come up with something new: show dates of events leading up to and following the Declaration, give a lecture on the Declaration and what it means, and have classmates play a multiple-choice game with facts about the Declaration.

Not bad, but she doesn't feel particularly excited about any of the possibilities. For one thing, she already used a couple of the ideas in earlier projects, and other kids have used some of the other ideas. It's much more fun to do something completely different—and more fun for the class, too. What I really need, she thinks, is something that *I'd* find interesting, if I were listening. What do I find interesting about history? *The people.* The reason these ideas aren't exciting is that they don't focus very much on the people involved, their lives and their feelings. But no new ideas come.

Margaret realizes that it's time for a break. So she deliberately *does not* think about the project for a day or two. Then, suddenly, while watching rehearsals for her class play, the idea strikes her: she will focus on the writer of the Declaration of Independence, Thomas Jefferson. But instead of talking about him, she will impersonate him. She will try to find out how he looked and spoke, make up some sort of costume, and have Jefferson speak to her classmates about the Declaration.

Margaret realizes that this is a somewhat risky undertaking, but she's eager to give it a try. As she excitedly gathers her materials and organizes her information, the plan is modified and refined. To give her class some idea of what Jefferson was like, she'll start by having "him" talk about himself—his upbringing, his education, his beliefs. Then she'll read segments of the Declaration itself. But, because the language is so difficult (she had to look up most of the words in the dictionary and ask her parents and teacher for help), she will take off her three-cornered hat after each segment and explain to the class in modern language just what it means.

With some stretch of the imagination, it does look a bit like Thomas Jefferson standing up there at the front of the classroom on the day Margaret does her presentation.

> My name is Thomas Jefferson, and I've come to visit your class from my life in the eighteenth century. I'm here because I want to tell you about the most important thing I ever wrote—the Declaration of Independence. But first, let me tell you something about myself. I was born on April 13, 1743, in Virginia. My parents were named Peter and Jane. My father made maps for a living, so I learned very young about countries, states, and counties. He made sure that I got the best education available in those days. . . .

After the brief autobiography, Jefferson introduces the Declaration of Independence. He reads a segment from a parchmentlike sheet of paper (burned around the edges, for that authentic touch), then takes off his hat and informally translates.

As she takes her seat, Margaret is quite pleased with the whole project, and she can tell from the smiles of her classmates and her teacher that the presentation was a success.

But was it creative? Margaret's presentation was certainly novel. It was quite different from anything she had done before and, in fact, it was unique within her entire classroom (maybe within her entire school). And, by any criteria, it was appropriate as well. She fulfilled the explicit assignment (teaching her classmates about her assigned topic), and she fulfilled the implicit assignment as well (learning new history material on her own). So, clearly, Margaret's work was very creative. And it is a perfect example of a child's progress through the entire creative process.

THE CREATIVE PROCESS: MAKING SOUP

Being creative is like making soup. Over the past few decades, creativity researchers and theorists have identified five main stages of the creative process. The first stage is *problem presentation,* where the task is set. This is when you are told to make some soup, or maybe just decide that you *want* to make some soup.

Margaret's problem was to prepare a report on the Declaration of Independence. She might have simply decided to open a can of prepared soup by writing a report made up of excerpts from encyclopedias. But she chose to cook up something fresh and new.

Stage two in the creative process is *preparation.* This is when you gather all the information and resources that will be necessary to solve the problem or do the task, when you go through the cupboards and the refrigerator to gather all the ingredients.

The third stage of the creative process is the one that most people think of as creativity—the *generation of ideas or possibilities*. This is where the cook puts the soup ingredients together in whatever way seems best: maybe mostly noodles, maybe vegetables and meat predominate, or perhaps it's a simple stock. Margaret generated quite a number of possibilities: making a chart of main points in the Declaration, showing names and dates of the writers, giving a chronicle of the main events, running a multiple-choice game, and—finally —impersonating Thomas Jefferson.

Notice that the process of *incubation* sometimes occurs in the third stage. Incubation means leaving the problem for a while, as Margaret did, and then coming back to it later or waiting for an idea to pop up serendipitously. This can be effective in reaching for new ideas, new perspectives. It's like letting soup simmer by itself for a long while; sometimes a new and better flavor emerges.

Stage four of the creative process is *validation,* the checking or testing of the different possibilities generated in stage three. This is where the cook tastes the soup. Is it soup? Is it good? When Margaret checked out her initial ideas, she decided that she wasn't thrilled with them. So she set the problem aside for a while, and later came up with a new idea that satisfied her "validation check."

As with Margaret, it often happens that a person will cycle back and forth between stage three (generating ideas) and stage four (validating ideas). The cook might mix some ingredients together, taste the soup, decide to try something a little different, taste again, and so on.

The fifth and final stage is *outcome assessment.* Here a decision is made to stop because the task was finished successfully, to try again because the outcome wasn't completely satisfactory, or to stop because there's no possibility of coming up with anything good! Margaret knew, once she had worked through her Thomas Jefferson idea, that it was just the sort of presentation she wanted—so she stopped there. If she still hadn't been satisfied, she might have gone back to stage one and tried to reformulate the problem. If she had made absolutely no progress, she might have simply given up. The cook can smile and prepare to serve the soup, or go back to the stove with a few changes in mind, or throw the whole thing out and leave the kitchen.

THE BASIC INGREDIENTS: WHAT MAKES THE SOUP SO GOOD?

Now that we've described the process of creativity, let's look at its contents.

The First Component: Domain Skills

Margaret is a very smart girl. At least, she is smart when it comes to learning history. It also seems that she has picked up some very good skills in historical research; she knows where to find the information and how to keep a record of it. These characteristics are all part of the first component of creativity: skills in the domain, or domain skills. Margaret has very strong skills in the domain of history.

Domain skills are the raw materials of talent, education, and experience in a particular area. In our soup metaphor, let the mind be a great soup kettle, and let domain skills be the different foods that the cook will use.

To some extent, domain skills are inborn; children certainly are born with different degrees of talent. But education and experience can go a long way toward developing even modest levels of talent. And even high levels of talent need to be developed.

It is so obvious that people need skills in an area before

they can be creative that we often ignore it. But whoever heard of a scientist who did creative work in nuclear physics without learning any nuclear physics? And no child will do any creative work in painting until she learns to hold the paintbrush, mix the colors, and make the marks she intends to make on the paper. Interestingly, an ability in one domain is not necessarily related to ability in other areas. So, it is misleading to call someone creative; we should always be specific about the domain.

Would any child with Margaret's education and experience learn history and use it as well as she has? No. In fact, many children, even those very motivated to do well in history, would not succeed to the extent Margaret has. Margaret's brothers, who heard the same nightly stories that she heard, have not developed any special knack for history. Margaret seems to have had a special *talent* for learning history, from the time she was very little, and that talent gives her an edge.

The concept of talent is an elusive one, difficult to define or measure. In some outstanding cases, it's obvious that a child has a special talent. It's clear that Pablo Casals displayed an unusual musical talent from a very young age. But perhaps the most extreme example of musical talent in a young child is Wolfgang Amadeus Mozart.

Johann Schachtner, a Salzburg court musician and friend of the Mozart family, wrote the following letter to Nannerl, Wolfgang's sister:

> *Once I accompanied your Papa to your house*
> *after the Thursday service. We found four-year-*
> *old Wolfgangerl [a pet name for Wolfgang]*
> *busy with the pen.*
>   *Papa: "What are you doing?"*
>   *Wolfgang: "A concerto for the clavier; I'll*
> *soon be finished with the first part."*

Papa: "Let me see; that must be something remarkable indeed!"

Your Papa took it from him and showed me a smear of notes, mostly written over wiped-off ink blots. . . . We laughed at first over this apparent nonsense, but by and by your father began to notice the main thing, the notes, the composition. For a long time he stood intently studying the sheet of paper, and at last two tears, tears of admiration and delight, fell from his eyes. "Look at this, Herr Schachtner," he said, "how correctly and in good order it is all composed; only it is useless because it is so extraordinarily difficult that no one would be able to play it." Wolfgangerl put in: "That's why it is a concerto; you have to pratice it until you can do it. See, this is how it ought to go." He played, but could just bring out enough for us to grasp what he was aiming at. At that time he had the idea that playing a concerto was synonymous with working miracles.

Certainly, without the special training and experience his father gave him, the young Mozart would never have known what a concerto was, let alone have been able to write one. But we can have little doubt that the boy brought some extraordinary musical gifts to this learning and experience.

Mozarts are seen only rarely, like comets flashing through the sky. Nevertheless, most children do have some level of talent in one domain or another. This talent, combined with good education and enriched experience, can give them all the skills they need to be creative.

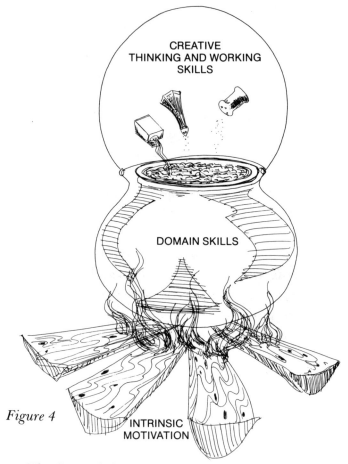

Figure 4

The Second Component: Creative Thinking and Working Skills

There are some special working styles, thinking styles, and personality traits that enable people to use their domain skills in new ways. These are the spices that give the soup new and interesting flavors. Some thinking skills appear to be inborn. But there are other aspects of creative thinking—such as working styles—that can be enhanced by education and experience.

Had she not used her own special style of working and thinking, Margaret could easily have produced quite an uncreative written report about the Declaration of Independence. But Margaret consciously *thought* about doing something out of the ordinary. She very deliberately generated a number of ideas before settling on one. When stuck, she set the problem down for a while. And then she developed a strategy for coming up with something that would be interesting.

A creative working style is marked by:

- a dedication to doing the work well

- an ability to concentrate effort and attention for long periods of time

- an ability to abandon unproductive ideas and temporarily put aside stubborn problems

- a persistence in the face of difficulty

- a willingness to work hard

Perhaps the word that best captures these attitudes is *craftsmanship*. Most people who do consistently creative work pay careful attention to quality because they feel a sense of personal pride in anything they produce. After the great success of his novel, *The World According to Garp*, it might have been tempting for John Irving to believe that he no longer had to work so hard. But he continues to believe in painstakingly trying to become a better and better writer all the time.

> I always had the feeling that I was apprenticed to a craft and a tradition—that I was learning my trade. The only thing that's changed for me is that, when I started *The Cider House Rules* [published in 1985], I felt the same way but much more strongly. For all the intellectualizing that is done about

novels, about the writing of fiction, I think the only part of one's writing that a writer can consciously improve is the *craft,* the technical stuff. It's really just the craft of the storytelling, the technique of the character-izations, the mechanics of writing. I think it's very important that you maintain a rather modest view that there is a craft of writing, and that you are always learning it —that there is always something you can learn to do better.

I am more and more conscious all the time of how books are made. They are made like houses are made: carefully, if they are made well. A good story is mechan-ical, in that sense. You can't simply be the architect and turn the plans over to any contractor. If you write a novel, you are the architect. You are the contractor. You are the plumber, the electrician, the roofer— you are all these things.

Here are some of the thinking styles that are often ob-served in creative adults and children:

- "Breaking set": breaking out of your old patterns of thinking about something. Margaret tried to do this consciously, realizing that most of the ideas she came up with had already been used in her class.

- Understanding complexities: appreciating the fact that most things are not simple!

- Keeping options open as long as possible: Margaret could have gone with one of the first five ideas she came up with, but she decided to let things ride for a while before making a final decision. Of course, it's necessary to start a project early enough to allow this luxury.

- Suspending judgment: generating as many ideas as possible, without evaluating them right off the bat. This is a key in creative "brainstorming." The idea is to avoid stifling a potentially good idea that might look peculiar at first.

- Thinking broadly: trying to see as many relationships as possible between different ideas. Margaret may have been doing this as she watched her school play and suddenly thought of dressing up in costume.

- Remembering accurately: the more you can remember, the more ingredients you have at your disposal for generating ideas.

- Breaking out of "scripts": breaking out of well-worn habits for doing things.

- Perceiving freshly: trying to see things differently from the way you or other people normally see them.

- Using tricks, or little rules of thumb that can help you think of new ideas: some examples, "Make the familiar strange, and the strange familiar"; "Play with ideas"; "Investigate paradoxes."

Some personalities are naturally more prone to creative thinking. The key personality traits of highly creative people include: (1) self-discipline about work, (2) perseverance, even when frustrated, (3) independence, (4) tolerance for unclear situations, (5) nonconformity to society's stereotypes, (6) ability to wait for rewards, (7) self-motivation to do excellent work, and (8) a willingness to take risks. If these personality characteristics don't come naturally, they can be developed in childhood and even in adulthood.

The Third Component: Intrinsic Motivation

What provides the heat that cooks the soup? What energy makes creative work actually happen? It's the third creativity component, intrinsic motivation—the desire to do something for its own sake, because it is interesting, satisfying, or personally challenging. As shown in Figure 4, intrinsic motivation is like the fire under the kettle: the hotter it is, the better cooked the soup will be. If the kettle has good basic foods in it—domain skills—and a good mix of spices—creative thinking and working skills—a nice hot fire will make a splendid brew.

Intrinsic motivation, too, may be inborn to some extent. But it also depends *very heavily* on social environment. This motivation to be creative has been so neglected that you might call it creativity's missing link. Ironically, it is the one component that can be most effectively used to foster creativity in children.

4

THE MOTIVATION FOR CREATIVITY

People will be most creative when they feel
motivated primarily by the interest, enjoyment,
satisfaction, and challenge of the work
itself—and not by external pressures.
This is called the Intrinsic Motivation
Principle of Creativity.

Being intrinsically motivated has four main
aspects: love (even obsession), dedication,
a combination of work and play, and a
concentration on the activity itself.

The greatest challenge for adults in nurturing
children's creativity is to help children
find and develop their Creativity Intersection—
the area where their talents, skills,
and interests overlap.

EVERY PERFECT ACTION IS ACCOMPANIED BY
ENJOYMENT. BY THAT YOU CAN TELL THAT
YOU OUGHT TO DO IT. I DON'T LIKE PEOPLE
WHO PRIDE THEMSELVES ON WORKING
PAINFULLY. IF THEIR WORK IS PAINFUL,
THEY WOULD BETTER HAVE DONE SOMETHING
ELSE. THE DELIGHT ONE TAKES IN ONE'S
WORK IS THE SIGN OF FITTINGNESS, AND THE
SINCERITY OF MY ENJOYMENT, NATHANIEL, IS
THE MOST IMPORTANT OF MY GUIDES.

André Gide

S ome children are, like Nathaniel, lucky enough to have an adult who tells them to look, first and fore- most, at their own inner motivation when they search for something to do in life. It is this motivation that will lead them to the work where they can be most creative. Gide encouraged his reader to use delight as his guide. In a similar vein, nuclear physicist Robert Oppenheimer wrote to his brother Frank when, at the age of thirteen, Frank said that he wanted to learn science:

> *Try to understand, really, to your own*
> *satisfaction, thoroughly and honestly, the few*

things in which you are most interested; because
it is only when you have learnt to do that, when
you realize how hard and how very satisfying it
is, that you will appreciate fully the more
spectacular things like relativity and mechanist
biology.

Both Gide and Oppenheimer are talking about the kind of passion that we saw in Pablo Casals and Isaac Asimov. Passion is ͺthat intrinsic motivation to do something for its own sake, the motivation to undertake an activity because it is interesting, enjoyable, satisfying, or personally challenging. It comes from within. Extrinsic motivation, on the other hand, comes from the outside. People are extrinsically motivated when they are doing something in order to reach some goal that is *not* part of the activity itself—for example, earning some money, winning a prize, getting positive recognition, avoiding punishment, meeting a deadline, fulfilling someone's else's orders, or getting a satisfactory evaluation.

A person's intrinsic motivation can vary a great deal from one task to another, depending on how interesting the activity is to him, but also on its social context. For example, a mathematically skilled boy might have no interest whatsoever in working through the problems his math teacher assigns each day. But he may spend hours happily working out those *same* computations as he figures sports statistics.

This point is an important one: there is no such thing as an "intrinsically interesting activity." An activity can only be intrinsically interesting for *a particular person,* at *a particular point in time.*

If parents and teachers can understand and apply the *Intrinsic Motivation Principle of Creativity,* they will have an enormous head start in fostering children's creativity. *People will be most creative when they feel motivated primarily by the interest, enjoyment, challenge, and satisfaction of the work itself . . . and not by external pressures.*

WHAT INTRINSIC MOTIVATION IS

Although the major hallmark of intrinsic motivation is interest, another is *competence*. Children will seek out activities, persist longer, and enjoy them more if they can get a feeling of mastering something on their own. And when children are told or shown that they have performed well on a challenging task, their intrinsic motivation increases.

A second important aspect of intrinsic motivation is *self-determination*, or the feeling that you are working on something for your *own* reasons and not someone else's. Not only do children need to feel that they are succeeding at something, but they also need to feel that it is their choice to do it.

Here's an interesting example of the self-determination principle at work. In a recent experiment, college students worked on Soma puzzles—three-dimensional wooden block puzzles that students this age usually find fun and interesting. All students worked individually. Half were allowed to choose which three of six puzzles they were going to do, and they could also decide for themselves how to use the thirty minutes available for doing the three puzzles. The other half of the students were told which of the three puzzles to do, and they were assigned time allocations. In other words, students in the first group had plenty of self-determination. Comparatively, the students in the second group had very little.

After the puzzle-making period had ended, each student was left alone in the laboratory for a while and told to do whatever he or she wished. The students in the "self-determining" group spent significantly more time playing with the Soma puzzle during this free time than the students in the other group. Also, when asked if they would return to the lab to work on additional puzzles, the "self-determining" students were significantly more likely to say yes. In short, they were more intrinsically motivated to do the activity after being given some measure of choice in *how* they were going to do it.

WHAT INTRINSIC MOTIVATION FEELS LIKE

How do you *know* if you are intrinsically motivated to do something? What does intrinsic motivation feel like? What does it look like to other people? What kinds of things does the intrinsically motivated person say and do? And how might intrinsic motivation show up in childhood?

My interview with the novelist John Irving answers many of these questions. Take, for example, Irving's answer when I asked him why he writes:

> The unspoken factor is love. The reason I can work so hard at my writing is that it's not work to me. Or, as I said before, work is pleasure to me. I work, and always have, quite obsessively. I can't just write for four or five hours and then turn the book off. I wake up in the middle of the night and I'm writing it.

This kind of *love,* experienced often as an obsession, came up also in Irving's description of other talented writers he has known:

> The funny thing about being a teacher is, ten or fifteen years later, the couple of people who really did go somewhere with their writing were *not* the ones who had struck me as the most talented particularly. But they had the best stamina. And they were obsessed; there was something that they wanted to do.

Interestingly, this remark of Irving's echoes that of the Nobel prize winning physicist Arthur Schawlow, who used almost the same words as Irving did to describe creative scientists he knew:

> The labor of love aspect is important. The successful scientists often are not the most talented, but the ones who are just impelled by curiosity. They've *got* to know what the answer is.

So one facet of the intrinsic motivation experience is *love,* sometimes even taking the form of obsession.

Part of this love seems to be an absolute *dedication* to working hard at the beloved pursuit. Irving objects to the notion that some people are "born writers," never having to really sweat over it:

> The so-called natural writer is just not going to get it done. At a certain level, the only thing that gets it done is doing the same thing, seven or eight hours a day, for two or three years, and getting better at it all the time.

Dedication, then, combining effort, self-discipline, and perseverance, is a second facet of what it feels like to be intrinsically motivated.

But does it feel good to be intrinsically motivated? Does it feel more like work than play?

> It's both. It was always both. And the better I become at writing, the more it is like both play and work. But I like hard work. It's a great thrill to be able to do what you want

to do with your life. Writing always tires me
out in a happy and meaningful way. Some
days it feels more like play and it is playful,
and the mischief in it is the best that's in it,
and other days you feel honed in on the
part of it that other people would call serious. But it's all serious, and it's all play.

So the third facet of experiencing intrinsic motivation is
this *combination of work and play.*

Intrinsic motivation is marked by a concentration on the
activity *itself,* and not on other factors. I asked Irving if, while
working on a book, he worried about whether it would succeed financially:

No, no, oh no. You can't, you *can't!* I know
some people do, but it's a disaster. The
book . . . that's where the obsession comes
in. When you're writing, you *only* think
about the book.

This, then, is the fourth feature of the intrinsic motivation experience: *a concentration on the activity itself,* excluding
other extraneous concerns.

HOW MOTIVATION AFFECTS
CREATIVITY

We know that self-determination—being able to make
choices about a task—leads to greater motivation. But does
self-determination *also* lead to enhanced creativity? A few
years ago, a student and I did an experiment that provided
some interesting answers to this question. We gave nursery
school children ten plastic boxes, each of which contained a
different kind of collage material (like purple paper triangles

or red lengths of braided yarn), and told the children that they would be making a design by pasting the materials onto a cardboard in any way they wished.

Half of the children were then told to choose any five of the ten boxes that they would like to use in making their collages. After the choice was made, we removed the remaining five boxes. For the other children, however, we pulled out five of the ten boxes and said, "These are the materials that we've chosen for you to use in making your collage." We then removed the remaining five boxes.

All of the children had about ten minutes to complete their collages, although we did not mention a time limit at the beginning. When about nine minutes had elapsed, we asked the children to finish up.

The twenty-eight collages made by children in this experiment were independently rated for creativity by eight artists. When we analyzed the scores, the collages made by the children who had a choice of materials came out significantly higher than the collages from the no-choice group.

Two weeks later, we set up a table with leftover collage materials in the children's classroom. The time that each child spent working with these collage materials was recorded, and it turned out that the children who had been given a choice of materials spent about 50 percent more time playing with these materials during their free time. In other words, those children had a higher level of intrinsic interest in the materials even two weeks after the experiment.

Can we somehow get people to *think intrinsically* or *extrinsically* about their work and, as a result, influence their creativity? The answer is yes.

A study I conducted a few years ago provided some striking results. My assistants and I recruited writers, using advertisements such as this: "Writers: If you are involved in writing, especially poetry, fiction, or drama, we need you for a psychological study of people's reasons for writing." On the average, despite their other commitments as students or employees, the people who answered our ad spent nearly six and a half hours of their own time per week writing poetry, fiction, or drama.

The basic idea of this study was to have the writers focus on either intrinsic or extrinisic reasons for writing, and then write something for us. We expected that those who focused on extrinsic reasons would be less creative.

Each writer completed a questionnaire about "Reasons for Writing." Some of them received a questionnaire that presented only intrinsic reasons for writing and others, a questionnaire that presented only extrinsic reasons. Then, all of the writers wrote a brief poem on the theme of "Laughter."

The intrinsic reasons were:

- You get a lot of pleasure out of reading something good that you have written.

- You enjoy the opportunity for self-expression.

- You achieve new insights through your writing.

- You derive satisfaction from expressing yourself clearly and eloquently.

- You feel relaxed when writing.

- You like to play with words.

- You enjoy becoming involved with ideas, characters, events, and images in your writing.

The extrinsic reasons for writing were:

- You realize that, with the introduction of dozens of magazines every year, the market for freelance writing is constantly expanding.

- You want your writing teachers to be favorably impressed with your writing talent.

- You have heard of cases where one best-selling novel or collection of poems has made the author financially secure.

- You enjoy public recognition of your work.

- You know that many of the best jobs available require good writing skills.

- You know that writing ability is one of the major criteria for acceptance into graduate school.

- Your teachers and parents have encouraged you to go into writing.

After the study was complete, we asked several poets to judge the "Laughter" poems. The results were quite dramatic. The writers in the intrinsic group wrote poems that were judged as much more creative than the poems produced by the extrinsic group.

Let me make it clear that this effect was temporary. But it is nonetheless striking. If such a brief-and subtle manipulation could have such a significant impact on the creativity of highly motivated people, just think of the potential effects of the "extrinsic" messages that come through in classrooms, offices, and homes everyday.

WHY MOTIVATION AFFECTS CREATIVITY ---

Imagine that a task or activity is a maze that you must get through. (See Figure 5.) Say, for simplicity's sake, that there is only one entrance to the maze. Say also that there is one very straightforward, well-worn, familiar pathway out of the maze—a straight line that you have followed a hundred times, and that you could practically follow in your sleep. This is the way you have always approached the task, and the

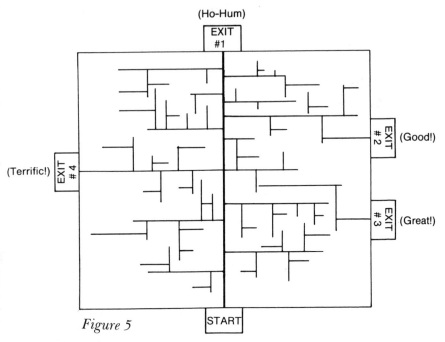

(Ho-Hum)

EXIT #1

EXIT #2 (Good!)

(Terrific!) EXIT #4

EXIT #3 (Great!)

Figure 5

START

way other people do it. By taking this pathway, you have gotten out of the maze—you have fulfilled the basic requirements of the task. In other words, you have found a solution that is adequate. It is also quite uncreative.

There are, of course, other exits from the maze—and these end points might well be creative, elegant, and exciting. The problem is that none of these exits can be reached from the familiar, straightforward pathway; some deviation, some exploration is required. Moreover, you'll be taking the risk of getting stuck in a dead end; you'll have to be flexible enough to back up and try something else.

If you are extrinsically motivated, by something outside of the task itself (such as a promised reward for finishing), the most reasonable thing for you to do is take the simplest, safest path—to follow the familiar routine, the conservative method. If, however, you are intrinsically motivated, you *enjoy being in the maze,* you *want* to explore it, and you will be able to take those dead ends in stride. Only then will you be likely to discover a new and possibly creative way out.

THE CREATIVITY INTERSECTION

Our culture places great emphasis on intelligence, talent, skill, and hard work. Certainly, all of these are important. But they make up only two-thirds of the creativity formula; the remaining third is intrinsic motivation.

In helping children to become their most creative selves, it is not enough for us to train them in skills or give them opportunities in which to develop their talents. Nor is it enough to teach them good work habits. We must help them identify the places where their *interests* and their *skills* overlap: the Creativity Intersection. (See Figure 6.)

THE CREATIVITY INTERSECTION

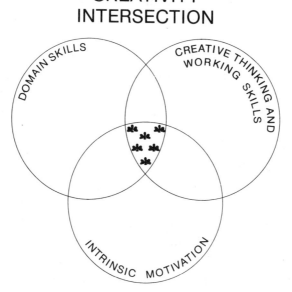

Figure 6

In this area, a child's domain skills and creative-thinking skills overlap with his or her intrinsic interests. It's a powerful combination, because *that's* where the child is most likely to be creative.

IS YOUR CHILD
INTRINSICALLY MOTIVATED?

Identifying children's intrinsic interests may seem difficult, but only because you're not used to doing it in any
formal way. Just watch your children, carefully. When left to
their own devices, what activities do they naturally seem to
gravitate to? Some kids will always be pounding away at the
piano; others will crawl off into the corner with a pile of
books or some crayons and paper; still others will be outdoors collecting insects. Intrinsic motivation is nothing mys-
terious; it's simply evident in your child's basic interests and
is expressed naturally in everyday behavior. Sometimes,
though, particularly with gifted children, it's difficult to
know if a child's interest is being influenced by some external
force. Kids like these sometimes do activities out of some
sense of obligation or some desire to win further praise and
reward.

Here's a test I have devised to help parents and teachers
identify intrinsic and extrinsic motivation in children. You
can use it in a few different ways. First, you can simply listen
to what a child has to say about a given activity, and see if
those statements more closely match the intrinsic list or the
extrinsic list. Second, you can watch a child carefully over a
period of time and try to decide for yourself whether the
child would say "true" or "false" to each of the statements.
Third, if you believe your child would understand the statements, you can actually sit down with the child, read each of
the statements, and ask him or her to truthfully answer
"true" or "false" to each one. Finally, older children can read
and answer the statements themselves. Of course, make it
clear to your child that there are no right or wrong answers!

THE I/E MOTIVATION TEST

This test includes sixteen *instrinsic* statements (marked
with I) and sixteen *extrinsic* ones (marked with E). Use the

particular activity's name (such as "dancing" or "making things out of wood" or "writing") in place of the phrase "do this activity." Each statement should be marked as true or false. If there are more true responses to the *intrinsic* statements, the child is primarily intrinsically motivated toward the activity. If there are more true responses to the *extrinsic* statements, the child is probably more extrinsically motivated.

I____ 1. I have nagged my parents so they would allow me to do (this activity).

E____ 2. I think a lot about the good things my parents or teachers will say when I do (this activity).

I____ 3. When I do (this activity), I feel that I am learning things I really want to know.

I____ 4. When I have the choice of many different things to do, I often choose (this activity).

E____ 5. I want my parents and teachers to know how good I really can be at (this activity).

I____ 6. I do (this activity) because I'm really curious about it.

E____ 7. I hope that someday I'll make a lot of money doing (this activity).

E____ 8. I like it when someone watches me do (this activity).

I____ 9. The more challenging (this activity) is for me, the more I enjoy it.

E____ 10. I do (this activity) because my parents or teachers have told me I have a talent for it.

I____ 11. I really enjoy seeing what I've done in (this activity).

E____ 12. I do (this activity) mostly because my parents or teachers want me to do it.

I___ 13.   I like figuring things out for myself when I do (this activity).

E___ 14.   When I'm doing (this activity), I think about what other people will say when I'm finished.

I___ 15.   For me, (this activity) is more like play than like work.

I___ 16.   Sometimes, when I'm doing (this activity), I forget about everything else.

E___ 17.   I believe there's no point in doing (this activity) if nobody else knows about it.

I___ 18.   I feel really good when I know I'm doing (this activity) well.

E___ 19.   A lot of times, I do (this activity) without really feeling like it.

I___ 20.   When I do (this activity), I like deciding for myself how I'm going to do it.

E___ 21.   I like it when somebody guides me by telling me just how to do (this activity).

I___ 22.   I'd be really disappointed if I couldn't do (this activity) anymore.

E___ 23.   I do (this activity) because other people have told me I'm good at it.

I___ 24.   I have a lot of fun doing (this activity).

E___ 25.   I like (this activity) best when I can do it easily.

I___ 26.   Sometimes, when I'm doing (this activity), I lose track of time.

E___ 27.   I really enjoy doing better at (this activity) than other kids.

E___ 28.   If I didn't have to do (this activity), I wouldn't do it.

E____29. I hope that someday I'll be famous for doing (this activity).

I____30. I discover new things about myself when I do (this activity).

E____31. I really want to get prizes or presents for doing (this activity).

I____32. (This activity) is important to me.

5

HOW TO DESTROY
A CHILD'S CREATIVITY

Children's motivation and creativity can
be destroyed if evaluation, reward, and
competition are misused, or if choices are
too restricted.

Rules that control, rather than inform,
can kill creativity.

*P*assion is not invulnerable. Even the most strongly motivated children can be seriously undermined by inhibiting environments and, as a result, their creativity can be killed. Where do we find such environments? Are they the hallmark of rigidly traditional school systems and old-fashioned, authoritarian households? Unfortunately, such inflexible and conservative settings are not the only culprits. Even those of us who have entirely good intentions can inadvertently create climates that are harmful to the health of our children's creativity.

The problem is that, in trying to help our children realize their potential, we try to coerce them into learning and doing. "Coercion" doesn't only mean threatening punishment or laying down strict rules; it also means overusing rewards and overemphasizing praise. As Albert Einstein observed in his autobiography, any sort of coercion can undermine the sheer joy of acquiring knowledge and using it creatively:

> It is a very grave mistake to think that the enjoyment of seeing and searching can be promoted by means of coercion and a sense of duty.

What are those "means of coercion" that kill intrinsic motivation and creativity?

FOUR METHODS FOR KILLING CHILDREN'S CREATIVITY

Evaluation

Of all the conditions that appear to have hindered the creative work of well-known people, the most striking and consistent is an excessive concern with evaluation. The poet Sylvia Plath suffered a severe writer's block when she was in her twenties. Her own explanation appears in her private journal:

> Editors and publishers and critics and the world . . . I want acceptance there, to feel my work good and well-taken. Which ironically freezes me at my work, corrupts my nunish labor of work-for-itself-as-its-own-reward.

Simply expecting evaluation can undermine a child's creativity. In an experiment I did with some colleagues, boys and girls were asked to do a "spin-painting" and then a collage. Half of the children made both without interruption. The other children, however, had their spin-paintings evaluated before they began their collages. Later ratings by artists showed that the collages of the nonevaluated children were more creative than the collages made by children in the evaluation group. It seems that simply having their spin-paintings evaluated led these children to expect evaluation on their second artwork, which in turn led to lower creativity.

You might think that the children who had been evaluated on the spin-painting were less creative on the collage because they became discouraged. Who enjoys having their paintings criticized? But their paintings were *not* criticized. The remarks made to the children were quite positive. So even praise can lead children to be less creative, if that praise makes them focus on how their work is going to be evaluated. And other experiments have shown that just the feeling of being watched while working can undermine creativity, probably because surveillance makes people feel they are being evaluated.

Reward

Belief in the positive power of reward lies at the heart of our society. Most people believe that rewarding a behavior will improve that behavior. But it's just not so. There are plenty of "hidden costs" in reward. One is the squashing of intrinsic motivation. The other, which happens as a consequence, is the deadening of creativity.

Two literary geniuses serve as outstanding examples of the negative power of reward. One is T. S. Eliot, who suffered a severe depression after learning that he had won the Nobel prize in literature. Shortly after the prize was announced, Eliot met a friend on the street. The friend extended his hand and said, "Congratulations on the prize, old boy! High time, I would say." Gloomily, Eliot replied, "Rather too soon, I would say. The Nobel is a ticket to one's own funeral. No one has ever done anything after he got it." Through his acquaintance with other winners of the prize, Eliot became convinced that this huge reward somehow became the prizewinners' reason for being, reason for writing. And that, he believed, immediately took away the personal incentive, the intrinsic motivation to write.

The Russian novelist Dostoyevsky was similarly paralyzed by reward—in this case, a monetary incentive to write a novel. In a letter to a friend, he complained:

> I worked and was tortured. *You know what*
> *it means to compose? No, thank God, you do*
> *not! I believe you have never written to order, by*
> *the yard, and have never experienced that hellish*

torture. Having received in advance from the
Russy Viestnick *so much money . . . !*

Interestingly, researchers have found that, for tasks that are very straightforward (like taking the straight, easy path through the maze), reward does help people perform faster and better. But for tasks that require insight or complex problem-solving, reward gets in the way.

For example, one researcher gave college students a problem involving a candle, a box of thumbtacks, and a book of matches. Each student's job was to mount the candle on a vertical screen. This could only be accomplished by emptying the tacks from their box and tacking the box to the screen. The box could then be used as a platform for the candle. Of course, the hard part here was seeing that the box could be used as a platform and not merely a container for the tacks. This is called breaking set—breaking out of a set way of thinking about something.

The students in the reward group were told that they could win up to twenty dollars by solving this problem quickly. Students in the control group, who were offered no reward, actually solved this problem much faster than students working for reward. It seems that focusing on that reward made it more difficult for students to "explore the maze" and find a new way of looking at the materials they'd been given.

Other studies have produced similar results. In one, students were given a series of mathematical problems, all of which—except the last—could be solved by the same formula. Students who were being paid for correct solutions took much longer to find that new formula then students who were not being paid. On top of that, the paid students made more mistakes.

The tasks used in these studies all required some sort of complex problem solving. Although problem solving is an element of creativity, it is not exactly the same thing. What evidence is there that reward has similar negative effects on creativity?

One researcher had elementary school children tell stories to accompany a picture book, either for reward or no reward. In this study, the reward was the chance to take photographs with an instant camera. In the no-reward group, the experimenter presented the picture taking as just another activity for the children to do, in addition to the storytelling. In the reward group, however, she told the children that they could take pictures only if they agreed in advance to also do the storytelling. Later, elementary school teachers judged the children's stories for creativity. The stories told by the unrewarded children were judged as significantly more creative than those told by the rewarded children. In another study, children's storytelling *and* collage-making were less creative when the children agreed to do these activities in order to get a reward. Finally, in a study with high school students, those working for reward wrote less creative stories than those not promised a reward.

Competition

Sylvia Plath was stifled by more than evaluation concerns in her creative writing. She was also fiercely competitive with fellow writers, such as George Starbuck (G.S.) and Maxine Kumin (M.K.):

> All I need now is to hear that G.S. or M.K. has won the Yale [prize] and get a rejection of my children's book. . . . And now my essay, on Withens, will come back from *PJHH,* and my green-eyed fury prevents me from working.

Competition is more complex than either evaluation or reward alone, because it encompasses both. Most often, competition occurs when people feel that their performance will be evaluated against the performance of others and that the

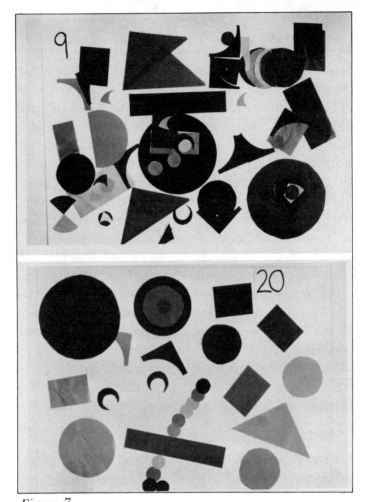

Figure 7

best will receive some reward. It's a daily fact of life and, unfortunately, it can murder creativity.

Several years ago, I invited all the girls between the ages of seven and eleven in my apartment complex to attend an "Artparty." I held two parties—half the girls were invited for Saturday and the other half for Sunday.

At the Saturday party, after playing some games with the girls, I showed them three prizes that would be raffled off at the end of the party. Then, I asked each one to make a collage for me to keep.

The Sunday party was just the same as the Saturday

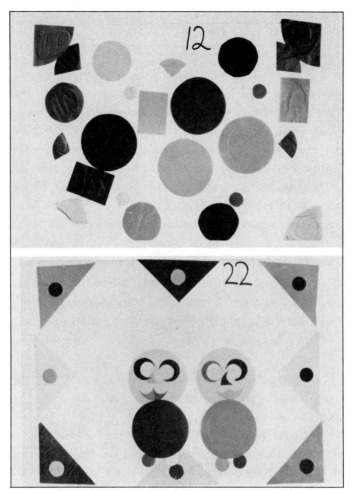

Figure 7 continued

party except that, before the collage-making, I told the girls that prizes would be awarded to the three who made the best collages.

Later, when artists rated all the collages for creativity, it turned out that the children in the noncompetitive Saturday group had made collages that were considerably more creative than those in the competitive Sunday group. Figure 7 shows four of the collages made in this study. Collages 9 and 20, both rated high on creativity, came from the noncompetitive group. Collages 12 and 22, both rated low, came from the·competitive group.

Restricting Choice

Albert Einstein felt strongly that learning and creativity could not be promoted by force. He had good reason to feel this way. The school he attended as a boy in Munich was strictly militaristic, stressing rote memorization and severe discipline. For Einstein, the experience of being told what to learn, how to learn it, and exactly how to repeat it back on exams was intensely painful. This is how he described his feelings after a particularly bad final exam period:

> This coercion had such a deterring effect upon me that, after I had passed the final examination, I found the consideration of any scientific problems distasteful to me for an entire year.

The destruction of Einstein's scientific creativity, though only temporary, is still remarkable. This was a boy whose fascination with science began at the age of five when his father showed him a compass. This was a boy who could hardly get enough of thinking and learning about scientific problems on his own. Yet, when thinking and learning were forced, in a highly restricted environment, even his high interest was shaken. Think of the devastating effect that constraint can have on children with ordinary levels of intrinsic motivation.

THE DILEMMA OF SOCIALIZATION

What's an adult to do? The standard tools we've relied on for so long in parenting and teaching—evaluation, reward, competition, and restriction of choice—can in fact destroy creativity. Do we need to abandon them altogether? And, if we do, how can we then successfully socialize our children into decent, responsible, law-abiding people? The answer is that we must perform a balancing act. We must use enough contraint to give children a sense of stability and predictability, but not so much that children feel the only reason they're doing something is because they have to. We can and should set limits on children's behavior. The trick is to set limits in a way that maintains their intrinsic motivation.

A beautiful illustration of this idea comes from a study in which boys and girls painted a picture after being given instructions about neatness. Children in the two *limits* groups were told to paint only on a small piece of paper, not the larger one under it; they were told to keep the room neat and clean; and they were told to wash and wipe the brushes before changing colors. But each group was given these limits in different ways.

In the *informational-limits* group, the limits were given in a succinct, sympathetic way:

> Before you begin, I want to tell you some things about the way painting is done around here. I know that sometimes it's really fun to just slop the paint around, but here the materials and room need to be kept nice for the other children who will use them. The smaller sheet is for you to paint on; the larger sheet is a border to be kept clean. Also, the paints need to be kept clean, so the brush is to be washed and wiped in the paper towel before switching colors. I know that some kids don't like to be neat all the time, but now is a time for being neat.

Children in the *controlling-limits* condition were given the same restrictions, but in a way that clearly suggested that the adult was controlling the child's behavior:

> Before you begin, I want to tell you some things that you will have to do. They are rules that we have about painting. You have to keep the paints clean. You can paint only on this small sheet of paper, so don't spill any paint on the big sheet. And you must wash out your brush and wipe it with a paper towel before you switch to a new color of paint, so that you don't get the colors all mixed up. In general, I want you to be a good boy (girl) and don't make a mess with the paints.

Children in a *no-limits* condition were simply given the painting activity, with no instructions about neatness.

The results were striking. Children in the controlling-limits condition showed considerably less intrinsic interest in painting later on, compared to children in the other two conditions. Moreover, children in the controlling-limits condition made paintings that were less creative.

What makes the difference, then, is not so much *whether* children are given limits but *how* they are given limits. If children feel controlled, then motivation and creativity will suffer. If, however, limits are given in such a way as to make children feel they are choosing to behave appropriately, destructive effects on motivation and creativity should be minimized.

By extension, the creativity-killing effects of evaluation and reward might depend on just how they are presented. Instead of simply saying, "That's very good," or "That's poor," say something informative, like, "You had a lot of trouble drawing the faces, but the colors are incredibly vivid." Instead of saying, "If you get an A in math, you'll get five dollars," present rewards as a *bonus* after the fact: "We're all going out tonight to a restaurant of your choice, to celebrate that terrific report card."

HOW TO KILL CREATIVITY AT HOME

The young woman seated before my desk was in tears. As this twenty-year-old's academic adviser, I was responsible for helping her sort out the mess she was in. Actually, it didn't look like much of a mess to the casual observer. She had been following a premedical program of study since her freshman year, with heavy doses of chemistry, biology, physics, and calculus classes. Her grade point average was 3.7 on a 4.0 scale. She had done quite well on the medical school boards. Yet, faced with imminent deadlines for medical school applications, she found that she just couldn't do it. "I simply don't enjoy it," she said. "Sure, I was always near the top of the class in those science courses. But I was never very interested in it. It was just a job to me, something I had to do . . . something I had to do just because I could do it! And I think medicine would be the same way. I know I'd be good at it. But I wouldn't be happy at it."

As I spoke with her, it became clear to me that the initial motivation for her premed course of study had come not from her but from her parents. They had seen this young woman's intellectual potential, even when she was a child, and had long ago decided that she would use her talents in medical practice and research—in their eyes, one of the most difficult and prestigious careers possible.

What she really loved, though, was something completely different. A couple of courses in "Psychology and Law" had ignited her interest like nothing she'd encountered before. Over the course of the next few months, this young woman convinced her parents that the field of psychology and law was best for her. She turned out to be right, and is now a highly respected (and very happy) practitioner of family law.

Out of a desire to help their children achieve as much as possible, many parents push (or coax) their children into areas where the children have little real interest. The end result is that the children may perform quite well by all the standard measures—they may get the best grades, win the awards, gain admittance to the best professional schools—but they will probably not be happy in that field or produce anything truly creative.

The problem, in essence, is that many parents do not try to find their children's Creativity Intersection—a problem that becomes especially worrisome with gifted children, who are often good at almost everything.

Home environments can also kill creativity by the inappropriate use of the four "creativity-killers": evaluation, reward, competition, and restricted choice. Here's a scenario showing how a couple of well-meaning parents, intending to give their children a creative experience, might instead do more harm than good:

Dad: Kids, Mom and I have planned a special activity for this rainy Saturday. You're all going to make clay sculptures of Disney characters!

Mom: Right. This morning, at the art store, we picked up this big hunk of modeling clay, and all the tools you'll need. We even took out your figurines of the characters that we bought at Disney World last year.

Susan: Aw, I don't know if I feel like doing that.

Sharon: Me either.

Dad: Well, how about this? How about we give each of you a dollar for each sculpture you make?

Mom: *And* an extra dollar to the one who makes the best sculpture!

Daniel: All right! Let's see . . . (grabs for Donald Duck).

Sharon: Hey, wait a minute. *I* want to do Donald.

Susan: I do, too! And I'm oldest.

Mom: Now, you kids should know that you're not allowed to fight! I'll just close my eyes, mix up these figurines, and hand one to each of you without looking. . . . Okay, Susan gets Mickey, Sharon gets Goofy, and Daniel gets Minnie. Nobody gets Donald.

All the Kids: Awwww . . .

Sharon: Dad, can I make a sculpture of myself, instead?

Dad: No, this is a Disney character sculpture contest. Come on, get into the spirit.

Sharon: Okay, but do you have to stand there like that, watching us?

Mom: We're just interested in what you
kids are doing. Looks like Susan's off to a
terrific start there—you guys better catch
up!

Dad: Hey, Daniel, you know Mom's rule
. . . you're not allowed to let any clay get
stuck to the table, and you have to clear
away the whole area before you can start
anything.

HOW TO KILL CREATIVITY
IN SCHOOL

I was six years old, in kindergarten, the first time I heard
the word *creativity*. My teacher had come to our home for
her end-of-the-year conference with my mother and, not
surprisingly, I was eavesdropping from the next room. I still
remember hearing Mrs. Collier say, "I think Teresa shows a
lot of potential for artistic creativity, and I hope that's something she develops over the years."

Although I didn't really know what creativity meant, it
sounded like something good to have, and I was thrilled to
hear that I had it. Unfortunately, my kindergarten drawings
represent the high point of my artistic career. I've often wondered what happened to that promised creativity.

There are at least two possible explanations. Perhaps
Mrs. Collier was wrong; perhaps I really didn't have any
special domain skills for art. The other possibility, though, is
that I *did* have the beginnings of such skills, but my intrinsic
motivation was undermined by the experiences I had with
art in school after kindergarten. Mrs. Collier's class had been
quite progressive, for 1955. Much of the day was spent in
free play, with abundant access to all sorts of interesting art
materials. I remember heading straight for the easel or the

clay table most days at the start of free play, and I remember carrying this interest back home.

The following year, however, I entered first grade in a fairly traditional parochial school. Here, instead of free exploration with art materials, my experience with art was limited to a closely regimented hour every Friday afternoon. Week after week, we were presented with the same activity. The nun gave each of us a small reproduction of one of the great masterworks in painting—da Vinci's *Adoration of the Magi*, for example, or Chagall's *I and the Village*—and asked us to *copy* it. This was an exercise in pure frustration, partly because the only materials available were loose-leaf paper and a few crayons, and partly because the artistic skill development of most first-grade children made any realistic rendering impossible. (I could never even figure out how to fit all those horses and angels on the page!)

Only once in my school years did I hear the word *creativity* again. Inexplicably, the teacher one Friday told us to take out our art materials and do whatever we wanted. I eagerly began making an intensely colorful abstract mosaic, not unlike a prisoner gorging herself on food after years of starvation. Sister, pacing the aisles, stopped by my desk for several seconds, then leaned her head toward me and said, "I think maybe we're being a little too creative."

What's worse is that we were also very strictly graded on the monstrosities we produced (at least, compared to the masterworks, mine looked like monstrosities). It was almost as if someone had tried to incorporate all of the creativity killers into one experience. Sadly, when I tell this story in speeches on creativity, I always find several audience members who had quite similar school experiences.

My story may (or may not!) be an extreme one, but all of the creativity killers can be found in both traditional and nontraditional schools, even today, and even among teachers who sincerely want to nourish creativity. *Evaluation* exists most obviously and perhaps most dangerously in the form of grades. By the time they are in second or third grade, most children have come to think of report cards as a very grave event. But, as we saw in the spin-painting study, even more subtle forms of evaluation can produce negative effects on creativity. Even if the teacher's evaluation is only oral, and even if it is quite positive, children who expect frequent teacher evaluation of their work will tend to be less motivated and creative.

Reward takes many forms in the classroom. There are gold stars, awards, privileges, and public recognition (such as reading a child's work to the whole class, or displaying it on a bulletin board). If children come to feel that these rewards are their main reasons for doing what they do, their creativity will be undermined.

Competition often occurs in classrooms through some combination of evaluation and reward. The most obvious form of competition is a contest in which some sort of prize is offered for the "best" work. But ours is a competitive society, and children will be comparing themselves to others and trying to compete even when the teacher does not place them in direct competition. For example, in one first-grade classroom I observed, the teacher did not assign children to reading groups but instead used individualized pacing for reading assignments. Still, many of the children competitively kept track of the reading books being used by the others, and developed a scheme for telling which color of book was more advanced. A friend of mine, twenty-four years after leaving elementary school, can still recite the progression of colors in her school's reading books—from "dumb khaki" to "supersmart aqua"! This kind of competitiveness can be quite detrimental to children's creativity.

Some form of *restricted choice* is, obviously, unavoidable in classrooms. Chaos would reign if children were left completely to their own devices. However, most teachers unwittingly undermine creativity by restricting children's choice even in areas where they could allow more autonomy. For example, if I had at least been allowed to *choose* a famous painting to copy, or if I had been given some leeway in doing an interpretive rendering (rather than trying for an exact one), my motivation for art might not have been squelched.

Teacher Attitudes

Research shows that a teacher's orientation toward control can have a significant impact on children's intrinsic motivation. In one study, children showed low levels of motivation if their teachers were controlling, and high levels of motivation if their teachers allowed them more autonomy. It makes sense, then, to expect that there will be lower levels of creativity in classrooms with control-oriented teachers.

Most teachers are familiar with the classic studies demonstrating the "Pygmalion effect": Elementary school teachers were told that certain children in their classrooms would show "unusual gains" in intellectual performance during the school year. In fact, there was no basis for naming those certain children; their names had been chosen randomly by the experimenters. Surprisingly, however, those children actually did show intellectual gains by the end of the year. Later, the researchers found that the same kind of gain occurs when teachers expect children to improve in creativity.

Rote Learning

During the 1960s, many proponents of the "open classroom" movement argued that traditional educational methods, which included rote learning of facts, undermined creativity. Indeed, some people suggested that too much knowledge is harmful to creativity; they argued that the most creative breakthroughs are made by people who have the least knowledge in a field. More recently, however, proponents of the "back to basics" movement have argued that education is fruitless if it is not based on the learning of a certain specified body of knowledge.

From the evidence we have about creativity, it appears that *both* viewpoints have merit. It is not possible to have too much knowledge to be creative. An increase of domain skills (which include knowledge) can only increase the chances of coming up with some new combination of ideas. It *is* possible, though, for creativity to be stifled by knowledge that is stored in the wrong way.

One of the wrong ways for knowledge to be stored is rote learning, or memorizing facts without any sense of how they connect to each other. Such knowledge may be very useful for getting good grades on multiple-choice tests, but it will be nearly useless for turning out truly creative work. Children who merely memorize their multiplication tables, for example, will be much less likely to think creatively about numbers than children who understand that multiplication is really a shortcut for addition.

Failure

All children experience failure at some points in their educational career, but the frequency of failure and the way in which it is interpreted can have a significant impact on their intrinsic motivation and creativity.

Obviously, failure is not completely avoidable, and we wouldn't want to completely avoid it. There are some lessons that can only be learned through making mistakes. But the way in which teachers help children interpret failure can make a tremendous difference. One researcher has found that children who attribute their failure to insurmountable factors like low ability will perform poorly and show less persistence. On the other hand, children who attribute their failure to changing factors (such as "I just didn't try hard enough") will persist more and perform better.

Conformity Pressure

Teachers are not the only creativity killers in school. Children can undermine each others' creativity through pressure to conform. The effects of peer pressure are obvious when we look at kids' clothing styles, entertainment preferences, and the sheer amount of time they spend interacting. But there may be other, less obvious effects of the pressure to conform. By about age nine, children exert enough conformity pressure on each other to dampen creativity. In fact, evidence of a "fourth-grade slump" in children's creativity seems directly linked to peer pressure.

Creative Children versus "The System"

It is astonishing to see how many well-known creative people hated school or did poorly in it. Of course, some did extremely well and appeared to enjoy school. Recall that the science fiction novelist Isaac Asimov performed far beyond his age level in most school subjects. Ernest Hemingway was a straight-A student. Similarly, the scientist Marie Curie was a star pupil as a girl in Poland.

Nonetheless, a surprisingly high proportion of very creative adults had miserable educational experiences. In some cases, the difficulty arose because the child lacked certain traditional "school success" skills. Despite great effort, there was repeated failure or near-failure. Two striking examples of such difficulty are Albert Einstein and John Irving. One of Einstein's first teachers told Einstein's father that his son was a "lazy dog" who would never amount to anything. In fact, Einstein seems to have had great difficulty learning verbal material. Similarly, the novelist John Irving was severely hampered in his schooling by dyslexia.

More often, however, very creative people had trouble as children in school because, in the words of my former teacher, they were "being a little too creative." For a child

with very specific intrinsic interests, and a high level of creativity skill (looking at things differently), school can be a
deadly bore. The writer and filmmaker Woody Allen often
skipped school as a child because he viewed it as a waste of
time; instead, he haunted the movie houses. The playwright
Lillian Hellman was also a great hooky-player, hiding all day
in her tree house and reading books until it was time to
return home. Mary Ann Evans, who grew up to be the great
novelist George Eliot, initially seemed to have difficulty
learning to read. But her brother later explained this was not
because she lacked intelligence, but because she liked to play
imagination games so much more.

What are parents and teachers to do when their potentially creative children chafe within the school system? One
answer is to try to change that system, to make it flexible
enough to accommodate a variety of learning styles and interests. Contemporary education seems to be much better at
doing so than the systems that repelled Einstein, Irving,
Allen, Hellman, and Eliot. But another possibility is to remove the child from the system. This was the charmingly
radical—but ultimately successful—approach taken in the
early 1900s by the father of Ansel Adams, one of the world's
greatest photographers.

In his autobiography, Adams recalled being in constant
conflict with institutional education in San Francisco just
after the turn of the century. He was extremely active as a
child (perhaps hyperactive) and quite easily bored; his parents had tried a number of different schools for him. In
addition, he seemed to realize even at an early age that rote
learning is insignificant, compared to "deep learning":

> Each day was a severe test for me, sitting in
> a dreadful classroom while the sun and fog
> played outside. Most of the information re-
> ceived meant absolutely nothing to me. For

example, I was chastised for not being able
to remember what states border Nebraska
and what are the states of the Gulf Coast. It
was simply a matter of memorizing names,
nothing about the *process* of memorizing or
any *reason* to memorize. Education without
either meaning or excitement is impossible.

As a result of his attitude, Adams was often in trouble in
school. One day, as he sat fidgeting in class, the whole situation suddenly appeared to him as hopelessly ridiculous. He
burst into uncontrollable laughter and was soon expelled.
His father, rather than chastising him and forcing him to
return to school, "concluded that my entry into yet another
school would be useless. Instead, I was to study at home
under his guidance." Those years of education under his
father's understanding tutelage were extremely fruitful for
Adams. The experiences that Adams's father gave him were
quite varied and always tapped into the boy's intrinsic interests in some way. These experiences ranged from learning
to play the piano to visting the Panama-Pacific Exposition of
1915 nearly every day for an entire year.

The words that Adams wrote in summary of this period
of his life stand as a lovely testament to the courage of parents who are willing to take risks in order to safeguard their
children's creativity and love of learning:

I often wonder at the strength and courage
my father had in taking me out of the traditional school situation and providing me
with these extraordinary learning experiences. I am certain he established the positive direction of my life that otherwise,
given my native hyperactivity, could have

been confused and catastrophic. I trace who I am and the direction of my development to those years of growing up in our house on the dunes, propelled by an internal spark tenderly kept alive and glowing by my father.

6

KEEPING CREATIVITY ALIVE AT HOME: SUGGESTIONS FOR PARENTS

Give your children a great deal of freedom, respect them as individuals, be moderately close emotionally, and place emphasis on moral values, rather than specific rules.

Create a home where: authority is questioned; there is a lot of activity, playfulness, and fantasy; and you and your children habitually try to do things in new, interesting ways.

*T*ender Places, a 1985 television drama, tells the story of a boy named Eric, who is caught in the middle of his parent's divorce hostilities. Eric witnesses one of many arguments between his father and his mother:

Paul: I think Eric should live with me.

Mary: Over my dead body!

Paul: A boy needs his father.

Mary: (sarcastically)   He doesn't need his mother?

95

Paul: Hey, you're gonna marry that jerk.
. . . You have each other. I filed for
custody.

Mary: WHAT?

Paul: Why should I be a part-time father?

Mary: Why should I be a part-time
mother?

(Eric walks between them)

Eric: Why should I be a part-time kid?

The boy on the right in the photo is Frederick Koehler, the young actor who played the role of Eric. The boy on the left is Jason Brown, who wrote *Tender Places* when he was just turning twelve. Not only was Jason's play produced on television, but it won an award from The Foundation for Dramatists Guild, and it prompted the *New York Times* drama critic to write, "Mr. Brown's play [—] is astonishing."

I wanted to know how a young boy, who had never before written a play, could come up with something so creatively well-done. So I spent a day with Jason and his family.

Jason is a highly motivated, curious kid who is eager to try new activities just for the experience. Although Jason had never written a play before, he had enjoyed writing comic books. His motivation came strictly from his enjoyment of *reading* comic books, and his desire to try something new: "I wanted to see if I could do it. I wanted to sit down and see if I could actually write something that I could enjoy reading; if I could enjoy reading it, probably other people would enjoy reading it."

His mother had shown Jason and his brothers an announcement of the Young Playwrights drama contest. "My mom asked my brothers and me if any of us wanted to write a play and I said why not—it might be a good experience; it might be fun."

Competitions—such as contests—can undermine intrinsic motivation and creativity. But Jason and his mother downgraded the competitive aspect and viewed the contest more as an adventurous opportunity. As Jason's mother, Carol Brown-Cohen said, "I was thinking, 'This is a neat little exercise and he's going to send it to New York and someone's going to read it and critique it and send it back and that's going to be a neat thing.' " Jason was excited about the remote possibility of winning the contest, but he wasn't thinking about winning when he actually made the decision to write the play.

"I thought, 'Well, this will be the first thing I've ever written in my life; that will be neat.' The contest and money left my mind, probably because I'm content. I'm not worried about anything extra." When I asked if writing the play seemed like work or like play, Jason answered, "It was both. It was work because I had to work at it in order to meet the deadline; otherwise I wouldn't have done it. But it was play because it was totally all my decision to do it or not."

The experiences Jason had early in life prepared him well with the skills necessary to write a play. He attended schools with programs in which children do a great deal of writing. In addition, he had acted in stage plays and in TV commercials when he was a young child, and had learned how scripts are put together and how stage directions are read.

But Jason's home environment and family experiences have probably contributed more to his creativity than any outside influences. Jason's parents divorced when he was six years old. He now lives in a middle-income neighborhood of Pittsburgh with his mother, brother, stepfather, two step-brothers, and numerous animals. Perhaps the most striking feature of Carol's child-rearing philosophy is her belief in using very little pressure on children. Although pleased with her son's success, Carol does not push him for even greater honors. "I think it's very tricky, because it's easy for children to get caught up in their successes. But it's even easier for the parents to get caught up and say, 'Well, I produced this great child and he's doing me great honor.' " Carol tells Jason that he is very special—but everyone's very special; everyone has their own special thing.

Carol gives her sons a great deal of freedom and encourages them to "break the rules" when it comes to their imagination and creative activities. At the same time, however, she expects them to follow certain principles in their behavior:

> They have all the freedom they want as long as they don't impinge on someone else's freedom. I'm more comfortable when the kids have limits, and so are the kids. It's important to set limits in *behavior*. I tell them, "There are no limits to your imagination, no limits to your creativity, no limits to your happiness, your sorrow . . . But there *are* limits on your behavior that you either impose on yourself or other people impose on you."

These messages have come through clearly to Jason. When I interviewed him and asked about his parents' expectations of him, he said, "I don't think they really expect anything of us as long as we do good things, and as long as we are self-satisfied."

There may be little pressure at home but, clearly, there is a lot of pressure in school. How is this disparity handled in the Brown-Cohen home? When faced with teachers who run rigid, punitive classrooms, this family takes two courses of action. First, the children are helped to accept the situation and adapt themselves to it. As Carol put it, "Every once in a while we get a teacher that's bad, just bad news, so what's the answer to that? I feel the answer is that there are a lot of different people in this world, and the kids are going to have to learn how to live with these people. Someday they may have a boss like this."

The second approach is escape. From time to time, the parents will play hooky with the children or, in Carol's words, "Do something fun to make up for something punitive that's going on in school." This is not to suggest that school should be taken lightly—only that school is not an ultimate, flawless authority.

Jason's mother served as both a model and a resource for him in his play writing. Carol had, herself, written a number of plays, one of which had been staged in Pittsburgh and had included her sons in acting roles. In describing his theater experience, Jason said, very naturally, "My mom wrote a play; she was a playwright before me." But it was not simply the *fact* that she wrote plays that was important. She really let her children see the dedication that writing demands:

> I always thought it was very important that the kids saw what I put into my writing. If I drove a truck, I'd want them to see what I put into driving a truck! It's important that they see me work toward something and finish it.

When I asked Carol if she remembered anything she'd communicated to Jason over the years about writing, she said,

> Just how terribly hard I find it to be. One of my favorite things to say is, "Oh sure,

writing's easy—I put a piece of paper in the typewriter and wait for the blood to appear on my forehead." Also, anytime I finish something, I read it to them.

In very concrete ways, Carol helped Jason by teaching him *how* to write a play, once he'd decided to do so. Jason remembers her advice well:

> I asked my mom about the structure of plays, and she said it's always a good idea to have the main character have a problem to be solved because then you have something to shoot for toward the end. She also said, write about something you know about. Don't write about something you can't prove or you haven't experienced.

As Jason worked through the first draft of his play, he often asked his mother for feedback (to the point where she felt somewhat annoyed), and she always provided him with a good sounding board. "She really helped me with grammar, and with how things sound. She wouldn't tell me what to say, she'd just tell me if it sounded right or not."

Carol is passionate about books, and has read to her sons and with her sons since the very beginning. There are books —many of them—in every room of the house, and Carol reads about five books a week. She says, "One of the first things I taught them—words are wonderful."

Carol is constantly offering new experiences to her sons (on the order of "Anybody want to write a play?"). When they were very little, she constantly engaged them in making up stories and songs. The family plays many games together, especially word games such as crossword puzzles. The children are not terribly restricted in how and where they do their creative activities. "I never made the kids go down to the basement to work with paints; I always had the paints around and they just did it." Carol also told me that she looks for opportunities to do something new and offbeat. "We had a flood in our basement and we lost all of our Christmas ornaments, so we said, 'Well, we're just going to make all of our Christmas ornaments,' and so we made them." The family works and plays together at pursuing new interests: "We have many different interests in this group. We'll get on a kick about something and go gung ho and get all the books on it that we can. We'll have fun with it and take it as far as we want, and then we'll go on to something else."

When I asked Carol if she has specifically tried to build Jason's motivation for creativity, she said, "No, except that I think he sees what kind of house we have—somebody is always involved in something creative, so it's almost a natural state. When you get bored, what do you do? You go and create something."

From the outside, the Brown-Cohen house seems rather ordinary. But inside, it is quite remarkable, filled with unusual objects. Here is my partial list of what I saw throughout the house: six typewriters (some of them quite old but still working); two computers; a piano; a pool table; a neon sign saying "OOPS"; photographs everywhere (including dozens of old family photographs); an electric piano; dozens of board games; hundreds of books; an unfinished wood door to the family room that has been carved with children's graffiti (examples: "Homework Stinks" rendered in several different styles, drawings of fantastic characters, "Abandon all hope, ye who enter here"); false teeth ice tongs in the kitchen; art prints on the walls in every room; oil paintings by Carol; a guitar belonging to Jeffrey (Carol's husband); a variety of bizarre postcards plastered on the bathroom wall; in the formal dining room, a framed painting done by one of Jason's brothers in the first grade; in the kitchen, a satirical essay written by another brother on "How To Be A Good

Kid"; a poster in the kitchen saying "Avenge yourself: live long enough to be a problem to your children"; a light sculpture and a pin-art sculpture in the living room; stickers all over one bedroom door; on another bedroom door, a beautifully lettered poster saying "The Wretched Hive of Scum and Villany"; two dogs; two cats; four hermit crabs; a fish; a lizard; and twelve snakes.

What kind of message do such surroundings send to a child? What impact does it have when parents give in and let their three-year-old son sleep for months in a refrigerator box that he has decorated, as Jason's parents did? Children who live in an unconventional, stimulating environment like Carol's home will learn to enjoy diversity, openness, and originality. Moreover, the opportunities for diverse activities (and the obvious freedom to *try* those activities) almost guarantee that children will constantly be having new experiences.

Carol believes it is important to look for the beauty in everything. She encourages her children to bring their feelings out into the open. But most important, perhaps, she has a vision for each child—one that is shaped by that child's own interests and temperament.

> The main vision I have for my children is for them to be happy. That's my goal. If they can be happy with themselves, I've achieved a whole lot.
>
> Jason was always wonderful. The vision I have for him is that he can do anything he wants. And I've *told* him he can do anything he wants. He has showed me a lot of what he can be. All of the kids have. I see each one's own strengths and weaknesses, and I go with those. The vision didn't start with me; they showed me.

Jason's mother has some advice for parents who wish to foster creativity in their children:

> Play with your kids; especially, quit instructing them. Just go with them. Let them tell you what things are about instead of you always telling them, because they see things in a totally different, sometimes bizarre, sometimes wonderful way.

HOW PARENTS' ATTITUDES CAN STIMULATE CREATIVITY

For over thirty years, psychologists have been discovering that attitudes and values in parents seem to go along with creativity in children. Of course, it could be that creative children lead their parents to adopt certain attitudes and behave in certain ways. However, when we put field research together with carefully controlled laboratory research on creativity and with psychological theories, we come up with strong clues about how parents directly influence their children's creativity.

Freedom

Parents who believe in giving their children a great deal of freedom tend to have creative children. Freedom-granting parents are not authoritarian, they don't constantly try to control their children, and they are not terribly restrictive of the children's activities. Moreover, these parents don't have a great deal of anxiety about their children; they don't worry excessively about their children taking risks. John Irving remembers his childhood:

> It seems to me a great luxury to be able to have as much time alone as I have. I could never get quite enough of it as a kid. And

yet my "space" was quite well protected for
me by my parents. They didn't smash into
my room without knocking. . . . I really
loved being alone. I had quite a lot of freedom.

Respect

Creative children tend to have parents who respect them
as individuals, have confidence in their abilities, and believe
in their uniqueness. These kids quite naturally develop their
own self-confidence for taking risks and being original. Mis-
ter Rogers is right on target: "You're special. I like you just
the way you are, just because you're you."

Moderate Emotional Closeness

Families with creative children don't have a lot of extremely close emotional ties. In fact, perhaps surprisingly,
there may be a bit less family unity and a bit more coolness
between parents and children than in less creative families.
It's also true that a child's creativity can be hindered by emotional atmospheres that are hostile, rejecting, or detached.
The key seems to be moderation: children should not be
overly dependent on their parents, but they should know
that they are loved and accepted.

Values, Not Rules

Parents of creative children don't make a lot of rules.
This finding appeared in a study that compared homes with
creative children to homes with less outstanding children.
The children in the "creative" homes had distinguished
themselves for work in areas such as sculpture, architecture,
mathematics, music, ballet, journalism, play writing, and
school politics. When researchers asked how many rules they
had for their children, the parents in these homes averaged

less than one specific rule (such as number of study hours or bedtime). By contrast, the families with no highly creative members averaged six rules. This does not mean that parents of creative children are permissive. Instead of making specific rules, they present a clear set of values about right and wrong, display those values by their own example, and encourage their children to decide which behavior exemplifies those values. These parents expect their children to act independently but responsibly. As one parent said, "I can't think of any rules we've had for our kids—we just wanted each to become a mensch [Jewish term for a truly admirable person]." Interestingly, most parents in the creative families remarked that they had surprisingly few problems with discipline.

Achievement, Not Grades

Parents of creative children have a high regard for achievement. They encourage their kids to do their best and accomplish wonderful things. Yet these parents define achievement quite broadly; they do not overemphasize grades. In the study comparing "creative" homes with "less creative" homes, parents of the former group said that "getting the highest grades"' and "having the highest IQ" were less important than imagination and honesty.

Independent, Active Parents

As a parent, your attitude about *yourself* is important, because you serve as the primary model for your kids. Parents of creative children tend to feel secure about themselves, unconcerned about social status, uninhibited, and relatively immune to social demands. They also tend to be highly competent and have a great many diverse interests both within and outside of the home.

Appreciation of Creativity

Very creative children say they feel strong encouragement from their parents to do creative things, and their parents say they are delighted to see their children exhibiting creativity. In the study of creative homes, parents cultivated their kids' budding creativity with lessons, equipment, and stimulating experiences.

Remember how Ansel Adams's father accompanied his son to the 1915 Panama-Pacific International Exposition, where together they would spend hours in the science exhibits. Charles Dickens frequently attended the Theatre Royal when he was a boy; his father entertained the children by telling stories; and Charles's nursemaid, Mary Weller, told him nightly bedtime stories filled with such terrors as black cats that drink children's blood and huge rats that are smarter than humans. Clearly, these particular topics may not have been the most appropriate for a young child's nightly comfort. But they did develop in the budding writer a real love of words, ideas, and dramatic stories.

Vision

Parents of creative children express a clear vision of their child as an independent, separate individual, worthy of respect and affection, who can be expected to act morally and responsibly in whatever situations arise. Moreover, that child is seen as capable of doing great, creative things with whatever talents and skills he or she has. This supportive vision can be quite specific. Recall, for example, that Pablo Casals's mother *knew*, at some level, that he would be a great musician someday. However, that vision was not her own fabrication. Instead, it came from loving attention to her child's special skills and deepest interests. The specifics of the vision must always be shaped in this way. As Jason

Brown's mother said, "The vision didn't start with me. He showed me."

Humor

One last, but potentially important, aspect of parental attitude is humor—the ability to laugh at situations, events, and oneself. One study found that humor abounds in the families of creative children. There is almost constant joking, trick playing, and family "fooling around." Family members often have comical names for each other, and use a vocabulary understood only by them.

Consider the somewhat zany attitudes expressed by Leah Adler, the mother of Steven Spielberg (who made such immensely successful movies as *Jaws*, *ET*, and *Raiders of the Lost Ark*). In an interview, she said:

> When Steven was growing up, I didn't know he was a genius. Frankly, I didn't know what the hell he was. I'm really ashamed, but I didn't recognize the symptoms of talent. For one thing—and he'll probably take away my charge accounts for saying this—Steven was never a good student. Once, his teacher told me he was "special" —and I wondered how she meant it.

SPECIAL EXPERIENCES THAT STIMULATE CREATIVITY

One hallmark of the lives of well-known creative people is the presence of various special experiences in their childhood. "Special" can mean anything out of the ordinary—

unconventional, rare, or particularly stimulating for a young child. For example, one Sunday when I was eleven years old, my parents said to my brother, my five sisters, and me, "How would you kids like to try writing some jingles this afternoon? The Catholic newspaper is having a contest for the best advertising jingle about the paper: they provided the first two lines, and all we have to do is write the last two. First prize is a trip to Europe for two! We'd really like to go, and we're going to write jingles this afternoon. If you'd like to try writing too—and maybe help us win the contest—we'd love to have you join us."

It was clear, from the beginning, that if *any* of our jingles won the contest, Mom and Dad would go. We felt very little pressure, and no extrinsic motivation. Yet it seemed like something really special, a truly different way to spend a wintry Sunday afternoon. So we did, all nine of us, sit down to write jingles that afternoon. And mine won! ("The *Catholic Union and Echo*/ Is our family's choice/ For it brings truth and guidance/ In an inspiring voice.") My parents got an all-expense-paid two-week trip to Europe (their first), including visits to the relatives in Italy and a private audience with Pope John XXIII. I got a tremendous sense of growth and pride—and a truly unique experience.

One common special experience is moving. Although children often object to having the family lift up roots and relocate, highly creative adults report having moved frequently when they were children. Because of financial difficulties, Charles Dickens's family rarely stayed in one home for more than a few months; they were always one step ahead of the landlord. It's likely that exposing kids to different cultures, life-styles, and attitudes, and requiring them to become flexible, adaptable people, inspires creativity.

The physical environment of a home can provide children with stimulating special experiences. Remember Jason

Brown's home? Here is how one researcher described the homes of children noted for their creativity:

> Most of the families of the creative live in decidedly different kinds of houses from other people. Some are modernistic; quite a few were located on rocky ledges in the woods, for example. Others are ancient; one family lives in a converted nineteenth-century town hall. Another bought a two-room eighteenth-century home, then added ultramodern bedrooms and a kitchen to the back of it.
>
> The insides of the homes were usually quite different, too. Many were decorated with surprising collections, such as Turkish teapots. In one home, a room was devoted to housing forty-seven unusual birds.

Often, the distinctive collections in these homes belonged to the children—campaign pins, for example, or models of prehistoric birds.

Your response to your child's new ventures can be very important. If you encourage and even help in such unusual projects, creativity can be stimulated. Jason Brown's mother gave him plenty of support and concrete help as he set out to write a play; she even typed the manuscript for him. Mark Godes, a thirteen-year-old advice columnist for the *Boston Herald*, got his mom to help with the typing, too. Recall how Jason Hardman's father helped him with his library project by accompanying him to the town council meeting and presenting Jason's idea. And young social worker Trevor Ferrell needed his parents to actually drive him into Philadelphia.

When Steven Spielberg signed up for a Boy Scouts merit

badge in movie-making, his father bought him a Super-8 camera. His mother describes what happened:

> From then on, the decor in our house consisted of white walls, blue carpeting, and tripods. My car back then was a 1950 Army-surplus jeep. We would load it up and drive into the desert. Steven had the whole family dressed up in ridiculous costumes. He'd say, "Stand behind that cactus," and I actually did it. I also supplied cold cuts.

Steven's mother was quite willing to go along with his outrageous schemes in the movie-making projects. When he wanted to make a horror movie with something disgusting oozing out of her kitchen cabinets, she bought thirty cans of cherries, cooked them in a pressure cooker until they exploded all over the room, and then spent years gradually cleaning cherries out of her kitchen. Imagine what might have happened if she had instead told him to go play outside.

CREATIVITY MODELS

> *Dear Miss Ellerbee,*
> *When I grow up, I want to do exactly what*
> *you do. So please do it better.*

This letter was sent by a young fan to Linda Ellerbee, author and television commentator. As adults, we can show children what it is like to think creatively and act creatively. It's very important, therefore, that we "do it better."

Two sisters, Sabina and Annie Yoon, published their first book—a collection of poems and essays—when they were just in the fifth and third grades. Being Korea's youngest published authors was not terribly unusual for them, however. Their father, too, had written poetry when he was in grade school.

Marie Curie's father, a physics professor, often invited her into his lab to examine his scientific instruments, glass tubes, small scales, mineral specimens, and other physics apparatus. He loved to talk to Marie about his work, conveying to her his passion for science.

John Irving's story writing was inspired by his father, but in a somewhat less direct way:

> My father is the first person I remember whose language was just better than anybody else's. He was very well-spoken, and he was very funny. I remember hearing him read to my younger brother and sisters —being quite impressed, listening to the stories that I heard from out in the hall.

Parents can also serve as powerful models to children in simply conveying confidence and competence. In her autobiography, the anthropologist Margaret Mead describes the impact that her mother and grandmother had on her own self-confidence:

> I think it was my grandmother who gave me my ease in being a woman. She was unquestionably feminine—small and dainty and pretty and wholly without masculine protest or feminist aggrievement. She had gone to college when this was a very unusual thing for a girl to do, she had a firm grasp of anything she paid attention to, she had married and had a child, and she had a career of her own. All this was true of my mother, as well. [—] The two women I

knew best were mothers and had professional training. So I had no reason to doubt
that brains were suitable for a woman.

Research has shown that creative children identify with
many adults of *both* sexes, and that frequent exposure to
interesting, active, effective adults can stimulate children's
creativity. Mead's mother made sure that, wherever the family moved (and moves were frequent), her daughter became
apprenticed to local people who were engaged in interesting
work. So it was that young Margaret had informal lessons in
drawing, painting, woodcarving, modeling, music, basketry,
and loom building. Similarly, Albert Einstein began reading
popular science books as a boy because these books had been
given to him by a young medical student named Max Talmey, who was a weekly visitor to the Einstein home.

Rather than shielding their children from new and perhaps intimidating experiences, parents of creative children
provide them with new experiences and the encouragement
to take advantage of them. One of the best ways to stimulate
children's minds is to bring interesting adults home.

All adults are potential models for kids: teachers, relatives, family friends, and grandparents. But the most crucial
models are parents. Be involved in creative work yourself;
concentrate deeply on it; take reasonable risks in your approach to living; show independent, flexible thinking; show
real self-discipline and craftsmanship in your work; and,
perhaps most important, place great emphasis on the intrinsic joys of whatever you do.

BANISHING THE
CREATIVITY KILLERS

In high school, I had a wise teacher who told me, "Don't
ever let school get in the way of your education." How can

you help your children deal with school in a way that will deflect its negative effects?

One of the strongest anticreativity forces in school is peer pressure, the influence that children exert on each other to conform, to dress like everyone else, to think and behave like everyone else. Begin early in your children's lives to help them be independent, responsible, and able to think for themselves. Encourage them to make friends, but don't be overly concerned that your children be popular and "fit in."

Much of the creativity-killing in school comes, of course, from teachers or administrators. As a parent, you can develop a number of strategies for overcoming these stumbling blocks. Obviously, the most drastic step is to find new teachers and schools. But, short of that, it can help enormously for you to simply become active in your child's education. Learn with your child, know what he is doing in school, show interest and enthusiasm, and encourage him to think about school subjects in more flexible ways. In his art class at school, Pablo Picasso was required to do everything according to rigid standards: this is how to paint a sea gull; this is how to paint a sunflower. Outside of school, however, he used these growing skills in fanciful, inventive creations.

If faced with a particularly inflexible or hostile teacher, you might try negotiating directly with him or her. Go ahead and show your child that you disapprove of certain things that are going on at school, but make it clear that he will have to adapt to them nonetheless. Jason Brown's mother taught her boys that having to deal with difficult superiors was simply a fact of life. And John Irving's father, when high-school-aged John would complain about the inflexibility of a certain teacher, would say, "Oh, *that* one! Well, you'll just have to put up with him or find a different class." The important thing is to convey that, although teachers must be respected for who they are and what they know, they do make mistakes and they can be wrong.

Teach your children that school is useful for gaining a great deal of important information and a great many interesting experiences—but that it is, nonetheless, a sometimes flawed system. Here's how Margaret Mead described the one year that she went to a "regular school" (rather than being taught at home):

> That one year, the winter of my ninth birthday, gave me a clear idea of what school was like. Before that I had known only about kindergarten, a kind of school from which I had never wanted to come home. In the first month of that fourth-grade class I failed dismally in arithmetic. But by the third month I had worked my way up to 90 percent in arithmetic and had discovered that school was a system you had to learn about, just as you had to learn about each new house and garden and explore the possibilities of each new town.

Certainly, creativity-killers are found at home, as well. It is impossible to raise children effectively without using rewards, evaluation, and behavior restriction. But there are at least three things parents can do to help: First, show by what you say and do that extrinsic goals (such as getting paid for a job) are *secondary* to intrinsic goals (such as a real sense of pride in a job well-done).

Second, use rewards sparingly. Take the focus off them whenever possible. Instead of relying on rewards and praise for your children's work, actually display and use what they create. Frame a special drawing and hang it prominently in the house; eat that pot of vegetarian chili . . . or at least taste it.

Third, show by example that rewards and rules can actually be used in the service of intrinsic pleasures. Explain that being neat in the wood shop means you can find your tools when you need them. Show that you want to make a good salary so that you can be free of worry about money, and free to pursue other interests in life. Tell your kids that, in the same way, if they earn good grades they will have more flexibility in educational and career choices. Show that promotions at work are important primarily because they give you more control over your life.

IN SEARCH OF THE CREATIVITY INTERSECTION

Remember: The Creativity Intersection is the area where your child's *skills* and *interests* overlap. It is the place where your child is most likely to be creative.

You can help your children discover their own deepest interests by encouraging them to try out a variety of activities. Present opportunities in low-key ways, then sit back and watch your kids take off. Children will often come up with their own new activities. As a nine-year-old, the future novelist Virginia Woolf started a newspaper in her home (the *Hyde Park Gate News*) and ran it weekly for four years. The readership consisted only of Virginia's siblings, parents, and other assorted grown-ups in the household, but their interest and enjoyment of the paper was enough to keep her going.

Children's interests develop and change over time. The creativity intersection is *not* a fixed point. If you are unsure about how "real" your child's interest is, it may not be a bad idea to test it a bit. Make the child fight a little for what she says she wants to do. But then, if she fights convincingly, give in!

Composer Aaron Copland nearly drove his parents insane hounding them to let him learn the piano—luckily, he finally wore them down. Seth Green, a twelve-year-old actor who starred in Woody Allen's movie *Radio Days,* announced to his parents that he wanted to be an entertainer when he was three years old. He didn't say much more on the subject until he was six and appeared in a summer camp production of *Hello, Dolly!* As he walked off the stage, Seth announced, "This is what I want to do for the rest of my life." After that he never let up, and a few months later, he complained to his parents, "You're wasting the best years of my career!" Seth's mother finally gave in and took him to a local casting agent, asking the agent to audition Seth and then tell him to "forget it." To her dismay, after the audition the agent said, "I can't tell him to forget it. No one is ever going to tell him to forget it." It was now clear to Seth's parents that he had a true talent that matched his intrinsic interest. Now they help him however and whenever they can.

Appreciating your children's intrinsic interests can impact in ways that are hard to predict. After Albert Einstein graduated from technical school, he had great difficulty finding the kind of scientific research assistantship he wanted. (He had annoyed and insulted a number of his teachers, and they refused to give him good recommendations!) On his own, while working at meaningless jobs, the young Einstein published an important scientific paper in a respected journal. Still, no one offered him a research job. Einstein's father, keenly aware of what a career in science meant to his son, wrote a letter asking a prominent physical chemist to look at his work:

> *I beg you to excuse a father who dares to approach you, dear Professor, in the interests of his son.*
>
> *[—] Everybody who is able to judge praises his talent, and in any case I can assure you that he is exceedingly assiduous and industrious and is attached to his science with a great love.*

*[—] Because, dear Professor, my son
honors and reveres you the most among all the
great physicists of our time, I permit myself to
apply to you with the plea that you will read his
article published in the* Annelen der Physik
*and, hopefully, that you will write him a few
lines of encouragement so that he may regain his
joy in his life and his work.*

STIMULATING CREATIVITY
IN DAILY FAMILY LIFE

*The older you get, the stranger your earlier selves seem, until
you can scarcely remember having made their acquaintance at
all.*

JOHN UPDIKE

*I'm sure memory and creativity are connected. Of course, when
you write, you use every resource you have. What other check
have you got? How else would you make connections, predic-
tions about yourself, or understand relationships—without
memory?*

EUDORA WELTY

Highly creative people seem to be deeply connected to
their past. They often have rich memories of the "strange
selves" they used to be. As parents, we should try to give our
children a personal sense of history, of what they were like
and what they did when they were growing up.

What does it feel like to live in a home that nourishes a
child's creativity? How do people in these homes live? How
do they interact with each other? What do they do, alone and
together?

In creative homes, parents really become intellectually

engaged with their children—they discuss things, question assumptions, investigate, explore. Parents and children look closely at the world together and become excited by it. John Irving's mother and grandmother spent hours reading to him when he was a child. Virginia Woolf's father frequently drew pictures for his children, cut magical creatures out of paper, told stories of mountain adventures, recited poetry, read to his children and then asked them to discuss what they had heard. And the physicist Richard Feynman learned much from his father's questioning attitude:

> When I was a child I noticed that a ball in my express wagon would roll to the back when I started the wagon, and when I stopped suddenly it would roll forward. I asked my father why, and he answered as follows: "That, nobody knows! People call it inertia, and the general rule is that anything at rest tends to remain at rest, and a thing in motion tends to keep on moving in the same direction at the same speed. By the way, if you look closely you will see that when you start the wagon the ball doesn't really move backward, but it just doesn't start up from rest as fast as does the wagon when you pull it, and it is the back of the wagon which moves toward the ball."

If you want to encourage creativity, *invite* healthy disagreement in the form of give-and-take discussions. Recall the advice that the physicist Robert Oppenheimer wrote to his younger brother:

> *. . . try to understand really, to your own*
> *satisfaction, thoroughly and honestly, the few*

things in which you are most interested.
If you think I'm wrong please don't hesitate
to tell me so; I'm only talking from my own very
small experience.

Perhaps just as important as the advice itself was that closing statement. Creative homes are often noisy and playful. It is through play that kids learn, challenge themselves, and discover their strongest interests. Research has shown a direct connection between playfulness and creativity: children who have spent time playing tend to be more creative on tasks they do immediately afterward than children who go directly from one task to another. The important point to remember in playing with children is to avoid overcontrolling. Even if your son is having some trouble figuring out how to do something, give him a little time and space to figure it out himself. Even if your daughter is using a toy in the "wrong" way, leave her alone—maybe she's just discovered a new "right" way to do it!

Parents occasionally feel threatened or concerned when their children engage in fantasy play. Who wants to have Darth Vader stalking around the house? *You* do. Fantasy play is normal and useful; it helps kids work out various psychological issues they may be dealing with, and it probably stimulates their creativity, as well. You can expect fantasy play to *increase* as kids get older, at least during the preschool years. Girls tend to use more "realistic" themes (such as playing house), and boys tend toward "fantastic" games (such as superheroes). Interestingly, the amount of television preschool children watch doesn't seem to affect fantasy play. Children who see a lot of movies and whose parents read to them often engage in a lot of fantasy play. Perhaps most important of all, children tend to view themselves as more competent, and they feel better about themselves, when their play involves a great deal of fantasy.

Do children who spend hours watching television or video tapes, listening to popular radio stations, or sitting glassy-eyed with rock music cassettes playing directly into their ears suffer when it comes to creativity? The evidence on the connection between creativity and exposure to popular culture is not very clear. Many adults worry a great deal about television. It may not be that the programs themselves are terribly harmful; it may simply be that spending all that time watching TV keeps children from doing other, more active, more creative things.

Most parents (including me) resign themselves to allowing a certain amount of television, music, and so on. But it might be possible to actually *use* popular culture creatively. I recently saw a group of children assume the characters of a favorite TV show, but make up their own situations and dialogue. I've seen other children put on elaborate stage shows (in the basement at home) where they pretend to be rock stars, complete with costumes and lights, lip-synching taped music. Children don't have to just sit and stare at the Saturday-morning superheroes; they can borrow from those characters to spark their own imagination.

Homes that nurture creative children are homes where both adults and children have "creativity habits." Very creative people have formed the habit of questioning what they see, taking new perspectives, finding new ways of doing whatever they do, and just simply creating as often as they can. As John Irving told me, "At a very young age, I got in the habit of making things up. I have to feel that I've had my dose of invention for the day." You can make creativity a habit by constantly asking questions such as: How can we do this differently? Is there another interpretation? What does this mean? What *else* might it mean?

A group of psychologists in California has carried out a fascinating long-term study of the homes and families of creative children. They contrasted these results to the homes and families of children who were not quite so creative. Tables 2 and 3 show the contrasting attitudes and behaviors of parents in each group.

T A B L E   2

Parents of Highly Creative Children

Attitudes These Parents Have

    I respect my child's opinions and encourage him to express them.

    I feel a child should have time to think, daydream, and even loaf.

    I let my child make many decisions for herself.

    My child and I have warm, intimate times together.

    I encourage my child to be curious, to explore and question things.

    I make sure my child knows I appreciate what he or she tries or accomplishes.

What These Parents Did When Trying to Teach Their Child a Task

    Encouraged the child.

    Were warm and supportive.

    Reacted to the child in an ego-enhancing manner.

    Appeared to enjoy the situation.

    Derived pleasure from being with the child.

    Were supportive and encouraging of the child.

    Praised the child.

Were able to establish a good working relationship with the child.

Encouraged the child to proceed independently.

T A B L E   3

Parents of Less Creative Children

Attitudes These Parents Have

I teach my child that in one way or another punishment will find him when he is bad.

I do not allow my child to get angry with me.

I try to keep my child away from children or families who have different ideas or values from our own.

I believe that a child should be seen and not heard.

I feel my child is a bit of a disappointment to me.

I do not allow my child to question my decisions.

What These Parents Did When Trying to Teach Their Child a Task

Tended to overstructure the tasks.

Tended to control the tasks.

Tended to provide specific solutions to the tasks.

Were hostile in the situation.

Were critical of the child; rejected the child's ideas and suggestions.

Appeared ashamed of the child, lacked pride in the child.

Got into a power struggle with the child;
parent and child competed.

Gave up and retreated from difficulties;
failed to cope.

Pressured the child to work at the tasks.

Were impatient with the child.

WHAT NOT TO WORRY ABOUT

If you can establish the right sort of home environment, your children's creativity may become remarkably resilient. It's natural to worry that various traumas, upsets, and tragedies in your child's life will stunt growth and creativity. There is some intriguing research evidence, however, suggesting that such difficulties will *not* necessarily undermine creativity. In fact, surprisingly, they may even enhance it.

In some studies, for example, the absence of a father (because of death or divorce) appears to be associated with *higher* creativity in children. One study showed that highly creative children actually suffered a greater number of traumas than ordinary children. And there is no evidence that early trauma *hurts* children's creativity.

Relax as much as possible about your children taking risks. As long as it does not threaten life and limb or threaten other people, risk can do a great deal to expand your child's sense of himself, his capabilities, and his interests.

And don't despair if your kid is a late bloomer developmentally. Early development is, in fact, a poor predictor of later creativity. If your preschooler seems less than brilliant, just remember one feature that the scientist Albert Einstein and the novelist Virginia Woolf had in common—neither of them spoke before the age of three.

7

KEEPING CREATIVITY ALIVE IN SCHOOL: SUGGESTIONS FOR TEACHERS

Children's creativity will be enhanced if teachers believe that children should be active learners, with a sense of ownership and pride in their classroom.

Avoid tangible rewards as much as possible; present rewards as "bonuses" after the fact rather than "carrots" dangled beforehand.

Give both guidance and autonomy; use learning activities that are unstructured within structure.

*M*y daughter, Christene, came home sad today. It was the last day of school, the last day of a year when she woke eager to get to the school bus nearly every morning, when she sometimes complained in the evening that the school day was too short. "It's just not fair," she said. "Summer is going to be *boring* after all the fun we had in first grade. Miss K. made everything so interesting. I *love* her, and I'm going to miss her terribly!"

As most parents of school-age children realize, teachers can have a tremendous impact not only on a child's educational achievement, but also on that child's attitude toward school and toward learning in general.

Similarly, teachers have the power to undermine children's natural curiosity, destroy their motivation, cripple their self-esteem, and stifle their creativity. In some ways, particularly good (or particularly bad) teachers can influence children more strongly than parents can.

I can remember clearly to this day the kindergarten teacher who always expressed enthusiasm over my paintings; the fourth-grade teacher who mocked my unsuccessful attempt to illustrate a book report; the seventh-grade teacher who called in other teachers to watch me give my presentation on Africa; the ninth-grade teacher who told me I was being "a little too creative"; the tenth-grade teacher who let me write and present a comedy version of *Idylls of the King*.

In a recent letter, a friend of mine recalled the profound effect one of her teachers had:

> *I never expressed a desire to be a teacher until I reached sixth grade. My teacher, although only in her second year, was outstanding. Why? Because she was creative and recognized our individual needs. She took a genuine interest in all thirty of us. She used creative writing techniques in 1962 that I have modified to be first-grade-appropriate—but still use in 1987! To say the least, Miss C. had a profound impact on my career and my life in general. She was my mentor before I was even aware of it. To this day, we are good friends and communicate regularly.*

Why do teachers have this power? Because they have more opportunities to stimulate or undermine creativity than parents possess. Many children spend more time with their teacher each week than they do with their parents. Teachers have the explicit job of evaluating children, and because children are so keenly interested in tracking their own development, teachers can become a kind of divine voice.

Can teachers really teach creativity? Teachers can certainly teach domain skills—knowledge and technical skills in specific domains such as the verbal, mathematical, or artistic. In fact, most people see this as the teacher's job. To some extent, teachers can also teach creativity skills—styles of thinking about problems, rules of thumb for coming up with new ways of looking at things. Such skills can be taught directly, but are probably best conveyed through example.

But what of the third component of creativity—intrinsic task motivation? It is impossible to directly teach intrinsic motivation, to *tell* children to be intrinsically motivated. Teachers can certainly model intrinsic motivation by freely expressing their own curiosity, interest, enjoyment, and personal sense of challenge. But the most important way to encourage intrinsic motivation in school is to set up a classroom environment free of the extrinsic constraints that destroy such motivation.

In reality, then, teachers can't really *teach* creativity any more than parents can. But teachers can allow creativity, nurture it, and stimulate its growth.

THE TEACHER'S ATTITUDE

The most significant way in which teachers can encourage creativity is to support intrinsic motivation. All children learn domain skills in school (some better than others), most children can pick up creativity skills by some exposure to models of creative thinking, but very few children get out of school with their intrinsic motivation intact.

Intrinsic motivation flourishes when teachers believe that children should be relatively *autonomous* in the classroom. A group of researchers had fifth-grade children read a social studies text under one of three different instructions from the teacher. The *Nondirected* instructions were designed to give children the greatest autonomy in reading the passage:

> After you are finished I'll be asking you
> some questions similar to the ones I just
> asked about the other passage.

The children had just read another passage and had answered questions about their interest, enjoyment, and feelings of pressure while reading that passage. In other words, children in the *Nondirected* condition did not expect that they would be tested on this second passage.

The *Noncontrolling but Directed* instructions were designed to give children a high level of autonomy combined with specific learning instructions:

> After you've finished I'm going to ask you some questions about the passage. It won't really be a test and you won't be graded on it. I'm just interested in what children can remember from reading passages. Read it in whatever way is best for you.

Finally, the *Controlling and Directed* instructions really limited children's autonomy. In this condition, they were told exactly what the teacher expected of them:

> After you are finished I'm going to test you on it. I want to see how much you can remember. You should work as hard as you can because I'll be grading you on the test to see if you're learning well enough.

The children in all conditions were later tested for their *rote learning* of the material in the passage (the number of specific facts they could recall) as well as their *conceptual learning* of the ideas in the passage (their notions of the main point the author was trying to make). In addition, the children filled out questionnaires assessing their interest in reading the passage, their feelings of pressure and tension while reading it, and their feelings while taking the tests.

The results were quite striking: Children given autonomy showed higher intrinsic motivation, less tension, and better conceptual learning. But this does not mean that children should be given no direction whatsoever, as in the Nondirected condition. Overall, children in the *Noncontrolling but Directed* condition seemed to do best: they were interested, they did not feel pressured or tense, and they did well on *both* rote learning and conceptual learning.

In another study, children who saw their classroom as autonomy supporting were also more highly intrinsically motivated for schoolwork, viewed themselves as more competent in school, and had higher self-esteem than children who saw their classroom environment as controlling.

In other words, the best approach seems to be one where children are directed toward overall goals, but encouraged to learn in whatever way is best for them. Always, the emphasis should be on *learning*, and not on *testing*.

What kinds of teachers are likely to establish a classroom oriented toward autonomy? They are teachers who have both a sense of their own imperfections and a deep respect for children. With this attitude, even teachers of very young children can help them become real *collaborators* in learning.

One teacher that I know is particularly good at supporting children's autonomy—and her students are highly creative as a result. Her approach is to offer ideas, suggestions, and guidance, but not to *give* answers and explicit directions for learning. She never says, "This is what your Halloween scene should look like." Instead, she provides plenty of materials and lots of encouragement for children to come up with their own ideas. Telling children to work *together* wherever possible, she stresses that each individual has his or her own unique strengths and talents. She shows them how to brainstorm ideas and nudges them to find their own way when they get stuck on a problem. Here is a typical event in her classroom: The children are making kites for a crafts project, occasionally going outside in pairs to test their designs. As Shelley and Elizabeth stand on the windy playground looking at how Elizabeth's "first draft" kite performs, Shelley notices the slits Elizabeth made in the fabric and yells, "You just gave me a great idea for something else we can try!" They run back inside, make a few modifications, and before long they have created a quite beautiful and functional kite.

Overall Teaching Philosophy

These are the elements of a teaching philosophy that encourages children's creativity:

• Learning is very important and very much fun.

• Children are worthy of respect and love as unique individuals.

• Children should be *active learners.* They should be encouraged to bring their own interests, experiences, ideas, and materials into the classroom. They should be allowed to negotiate their daily work goals with the teacher, and should be given autonomy in deciding how to achieve them.

• Children should feel both comfortable and stimulated in their classroom. Tension and pressure should be absent.

• Children should have a sense of *ownership* and *pride* in their classroom. They should be involved in setting up and maintaining it. They should be encouraged to bring materials from home (even "junk") that can be used in educational activities. Teachers should say, "This isn't *my* classroom, it's *our* classroom!"

• Teachers are *resources,* not policemen, drill sergeants, or gods. Children should be respectful of teachers, but they should be comfortable with teachers, too. Little robots don't learn, and they certainly aren't creative.

• Teachers are smart, but are not perfect.

- Children should feel free to discuss problems openly with both the teacher and their peers. This is *their* classroom, and they share the responsibility for helping it run smoothly.

- Cooperation is always preferable to competition.

- Learning experiences should be as close to children's real-world experiences as possible. Children should have both power and responsibility in the classroom.

THE CLASSROOM SETUP

The most obvious contrast between classroom styles in the past thirty years has been between "open" and "traditional" classrooms. Although open classrooms take many different forms, they generally have a less rigid structure, fewer constraints on student performance, and more individualized attention. The open classroom movement of the 1960s was heralded by some as the best way (maybe the only way) to foster significant learning and creativity in children. What does the evidence show?

Research reveals a puzzling pattern. Most of the studies conducted before 1975 indicate that open classrooms are superior to traditional classrooms in promoting creativity. Most of the studies conducted after 1975 show little difference. It's likely that over the past fifteen years or so, standard (or "traditional") American schools have gradually become more "open," so that the distinction between the two has become more and more blurred. Gradually, there has been more emphasis on student autonomy, fewer constraints, and less rigid classroom structures. From the standpoint of creativity, this is very good news.

One of the most important lessons learned from the open classroom movement is the positive power of individualized instruction. Children learn better if the level and pacing of the curriculum fits their strengths and weaknesses.

Children's learning styles are at least as different as their clothing styles, and much less subject to change.

But the best feature of individualized instruction is that it builds on each child's unique set of interests and experiences. Let's say that Eric comes to school terribly excited about the trip he made to the natural history museum over the weekend. If he is allowed to write that week's composition about the fossils he saw, his work will almost certainly be better and more creative than it would if he, along with the rest of the class, is told to write about some "one-size-fits-all" topic. His writing skills will develop just the same, but his intrinsic motivation will skyrocket.

Children are likely to become more flexible in their outlook if they are grouped by mixed ability levels and personality styles. With appropriate support from their teacher, they will begin to see that each individual has strengths as well as particular weaknesses. They will learn that different ways of approaching tasks can be equally valid. Ideally, they will learn tolerance of diversity, one of the prime characteristics of creative people.

In addition, the classroom should be as visually stimulating as possible (without being distracting!). Students should be able to look around and see an abundance of work products, materials, and scenes. And these should come from the students themselves. There should be essays and drawings, puzzles and pictures supplied by all children. Children should be allowed to choose the pieces of their work for display, and change them if they wish.

Diverse educational materials should be abundantly available throughout the classroom—and they don't have to be standard educational materials purchased through official school catalogs. The "science center" in the room might have a number of different materials for demonstrating and experimenting with magnetic attraction—a compass, iron filings, a magnet, paper clips. The "reading center" might display a number of books and articles, at different reading levels, on a given topic (such as space travel)—as well as stories the children themselves have written about that topic. For young children especially, an "activity center," where they can play and experiment with various materials, can be an important educational hub. One week the activity table might have magnets that the children can play with before they begin to learn about magnetic forces. Another week, they might be able to make a variety of arts and crafts from the beads that will later appear in a counting activity at the math center. Children should supply materials for the classroom. They can bring ordinary objects from home, or they can make materials to share. In one classroom I observed, for example, Peter came in with a board game he had created from odd buttons, wooden spools, and an old tray. He showed the other children how to play it, then helped the teacher set up an area at the activity table where they could bring in "junk" from home to create their own games.

DAILY TEACHING STRATEGIES

There are a number of specific strategies that can enhance creativity in everyday teaching activities.

Evaluation

Teacher evaluation of student work is probably the greatest creativity-killer in the classroom. Having made that bald statement many times to my university students, I then proceed somewhat sheepishly to give them course requirements and letter grades—as demanded by "the system." What's a teacher to do?

First, use constructive, meaningful feedback instead of vague, abstract evaluation. Second, involve students in evaluating their own work and learning from their own mistakes. Third, place the emphasis on *"What did you learn?"* instead of *"How did you do?"*

According to the traditional educational model, teachers give students tests and assignments that are corrected and returned with a grade of some sort and (perhaps) checkmarks by wrong answers or mistakes. At the end of each grading period, the student brings home a report card with a summary grade for each school subject. And finally, the parents come in for a conference with the teacher at least once a year to discuss the student's progress.

In classrooms that support creativity, teachers assess students' knowledge and progress through ongoing interaction with the students. Students' papers are returned with plenty of comments from the teacher, highlighting particularly good *and* poor aspects of the students' work. Periodically, teachers send home comments about the students' progress, accompanied by summary grades (if those are required by the system). Before writing out these home reports, teachers have individual conferences *with the students,* giving the teacher's perspective on each student's work, soliciting the student's own views, and formulating new learning goals with that student. The teacher's written comments and oral comments to the parents would, ideally, incorporate the student's own views.

This system can make evaluation *informational* rather than *controlling.* Students then begin to see the teacher's comments not as rewards and punishments designed to control them, but as useful information on their own learning and performance. When this happens, intrinsic motivation and creativity will not be undermined; they may actually be enhanced.

Here's an example from my daughter Christene's first-grade work. Her teacher, instead of marking answers "correct" or "incorrect," would make an arrow pointing toward particular parts of a student's paper that required further attention. Sometimes the arrow would point toward a mistake the student had made. Other times, the arrow would highlight a blank that the student forgot to fill in or a set of

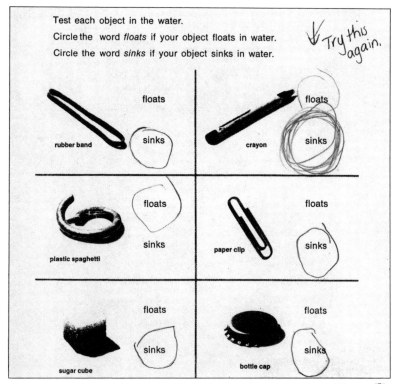

Figure 8

instructions that the student had misunderstood. In any case, the teacher told her students from the beginning of the year that an arrow simply meant "Look again." If, after looking again, they were still confused, she encouraged them to talk with her about it.

Figure 8 shows a science paper that my daughter brought home. The experiment that each child performed was designed to discover if each of a variety of objects can float. For whatever reason (because she misread the words, circled the wrong one by accident, or didn't really use a crayon), Christene marked down that a crayon floats. Her teacher returned the paper with comments designed to make Christene think further about the problem, not to make her feel criticized: constructive, meaningful feedback instead of vague, abstract evaluation.

Because most teachers don't really enjoy evaluating students' work anyway, here is a guideline that should be pain-

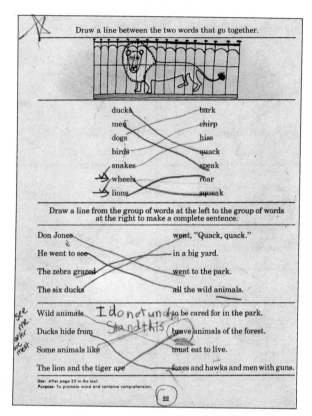

Figure 9

less to implement: Make the students do the evaluating. Enlist them as active participants in looking at their own work, deciding what they like and what they don't like, and trying again. Students usually know when they don't know something. The trick is for teachers to help students pinpoint, express, and seek clarification for their confusion, rather than try to hide it. On the reading exercise shown in Figure 9, Christene had a particularly difficult time. Because her teacher had encouraged the children to ask for help when they were in trouble, Christene wrote a note on the paper: "I do not understand this." Her teacher, after looking over the paper, wrote a message back; they would discuss the problem later that day. This sort of interaction accomplishes a number of things: the child learns to pay attention to her own learning process, the child takes an active role in solving problems, the teacher gets a clear picture of where the child is having difficulty, and the child gets extra practice in reading and writing by exchanging notes with her teacher!

Christene's teacher also found a way to help students feel better when they'd done particularly poorly on a piece of work. If, for example, a child had gotten nearly all of the addition problems wrong, the teacher would often draw a star or a heart next to an especially well-written number on the sheet. Then, when meeting with the student, she might say, "Yes, it's true that you had trouble with these questions. We'll talk about that and see if we can find other ways for you to understand it. But just take a minute to look at this six you made; this is about the most gorgeous six I've ever seen!"

In time, the children began to use this device in evaluating their own work. Christene would often bring home papers where she had, herself, drawn a star or a heart by a letter or number that particularly pleased her; sometimes she would remark on one that she "aspashly" loved. (See Figures 10 and 11.) Her teacher encouraged this sort of self-evaluation; from time to time, she would express agreement with Christene's self-congratulatory marks. (See Figure 10.) The children in this class also learned to point out their mistakes, however. In Figure 12 you'll see a paper where Christene said "Woops!" to an ommission error she made.

Occasionally, children are excessively severe in evaluating their own work. This can be a particular problem with "little perfectionists," children who are accustomed to doing everything well in school. These children might come to you with something they did—a drawing, for example—and say, "This is terrible! It's ugly! I hate it! What do you think?" If the child is really discouraged, it might help to point out one or two features of the work that are particularly good, or brainstorm ideas for improvement with the child. It might even be helpful to suggest setting the project aside for a while and coming back to it later. If the child is suffering

Figure 10

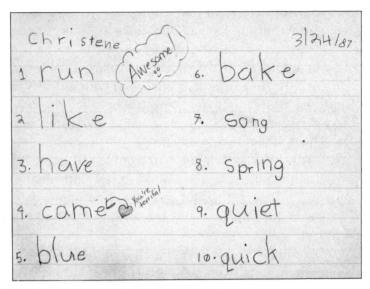

Figure 11

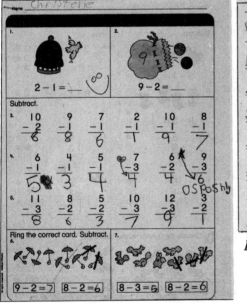

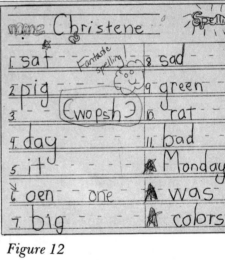

Figure 12

from low self-esteem or a need for special attention at that moment, the very negative self-evaluation might simply be a bid for some TLC.

Some children need to be encouraged to use self-evaluation, especially older children who may have learned in earlier grades to rely only on the teacher's assessment. This dependency can best be changed by gently, consistently insisting that children think about their own standards for work and decide whether they are meeting them. If the child repeatedly asks, "Do you like what I've done?" you can reply, "Do *you* like it? What do you like best about it? What would you like to change?" This is especially important in areas such as art and composition, where there are few objective standards of correct and incorrect.

In all classroom evaluation, put the emphasis on "What did you learn?" instead of "How did you do?" One way to do this is to avoid formal tests—or to avoid calling them tests. Even before they enter school, young children have developed a negative, frightened attitude toward tests (perhaps from TV, movies, and older children). The word itself establishes a sense of threatening evaluation, no matter how you are going to use the test. Christene's teacher gave spelling tests all year without using the word once; she called them dictations.

Avoid continual negative comments. Instead of saying, "You missed that one again!" or "Won't you ever get this right?" you might say, "Can you think of another way to try this?" or "Let me show you another way of doing this." Quite often, children are aware of what they need to change; all they need is to have the error pointed out to them.

The important point is for students to understand the value of mistakes. The message is that mistakes are good, that they are instructive, that they are an excellent way to learn. Ideally, children will not try to hide their mistakes or be embarrassed by them.

Surveillance is closely related to evaluation. According

to the traditional model of education, teachers carefully monitored students' work. Did you finish the assignment? How many pages of the workbook did you complete? Have you started your social studies project? But in a model more conducive to intrinsic motivation and creativity, children are largely responsible for monitoring their own work. The teacher will give them goals to accomplish in particular areas within a given time period (say, a day or a week), but the children will have autonomy in deciding exactly how to accomplish those goals, and they will have responsibility for keeping track of their progress toward the goals. A daily or weekly checklist could be useful for this purpose. (See Figure 13.) Work goals should be arrived at collaboratively by the teacher and the individual student.

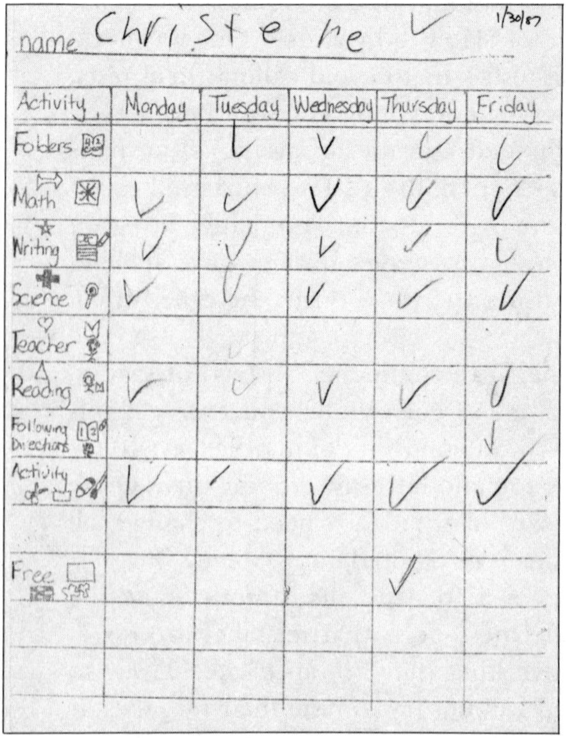
name Christene ✓ 1/30/87

Activity	Monday	Tuesday	Wednesday	Thursday	Friday
Folders		✓	✓	✓	✓
Math	✓	✓	✓	✓	✓
Writing	✓	✓	✓	✓	✓
Science	✓	✓	✓	✓	✓
Teacher					
Reading	✓	✓	✓	✓	✓
Following Directions					✓
Activity	✓	✓	✓	✓	✓
Free				✓	

Figure 13

Figure 14

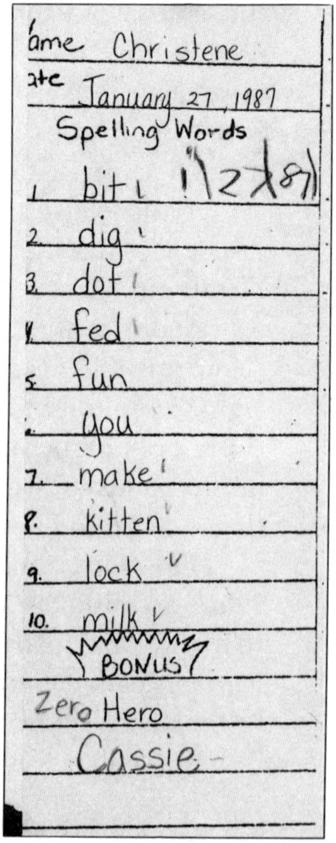
Name Christene
Date January 27, 1987
Spelling Words
1. bit 1/27/87
2. dig
3. dot
4. fed
5. fun
6. you
7. make
8. kitten
9. lock
10. milk
BONUS
Zero Hero
Cassie

Reward

Grades not only act as evaluative devices in classrooms, they also serve as rewards (or punishments). Other commonly used sources of reward are stickers, gold stars, awards, prizes, and special privileges. Children love such rewards and will sometimes do *anything* to get them. And that's the problem. Research has abundantly shown that when children become focused on reward as their reason for doing something, their intrinsic motivation and creativity will decline.

The best rewards for good classroom work are the intangibles: a smile or nod, a pat on the back, a word of encouragement, a chance to display and present one's own work, and additional work. Yes, additional work! If children are in a classroom atmosphere where everyone (starting with the teacher) believes that learning is exciting and fun, extra work can be a reward. The spelling list that my daughter brought home each week in first grade had the ten words required by the standard curriculum, but it also had two or three extra words at the bottom under the heading "Bonus." (See Figure 14.) In collaboration with the child, the teacher would write out extra words of special importance—words that the child really wanted to write correctly (such as the name of a close friend). These bonus words were like dessert to the children; not something extra that they *had* to learn, but something extra that they *got* to learn.

Another excellent "nontangible" is allowing children to express and share their own pride in their work. I know one teacher, very interested in students' writing skills, who held an "Authors' Hour" once or twice a week. Students would sign up for time slots in the Authors' Hour, during which they would have the opportunity to sit in the Author's Chair (a kind of film director's chair) and read their most recent creative writing to the class. This would be followed by a period of commentary and suggestions from the class (with at least some positive comments being required!), which the author would use in doing revisions. The process was a mutually supportive one, and because the reward (public presentation) was so closely tied to the actual activity of writing, it only added to intrinsic motivation and creativity.

When tangible rewards such as stickers and special privileges are used, they should come as a surprise to the children—an extra bonus because they have done an especially good job at something, or because they have tackled something particularly difficult, or simply because the teacher was in the mood to share something special with them! The trick is to use tangible rewards in such a way that students do not come to expect them and work explicitly toward them.

Finally, when you do give rewards, give them for creativity as well as for correct work. In this way, your children will clearly get the message that creativity is allowed, encouraged, and *valued* in the classroom.

Choice

Give children choice wherever possible. For example, a science lesson should provide a number of different objects with which to experiment. An art activity should present as many different kinds of materials as possible. When writing, kids should choose their own topics. Recall the maze metaphor. If children are presented with just one particular way of doing something, they will become like the rat in the maze who habitually takes the straight, uncomplicated, and uncreative way out.

The key is to have learning activities that are unstructured within structure. Children, especially younger ones, do need to have a sense of goals. They need limits, and they often need a general outline of how to accomplish the task. Within those limits, though, the more choice they have in exactly how and when to achieve the goal, the better.

Motivating the Unmotivated

Arthur's aptitude tests place him well above his grade level in nearly all areas. Yet, he did very poorly in the first few weeks of fourth grade, spending most of his time staring out the window or doodling pictures of baseball players or passing notes to his friends about the previous night's game. Realizing that Arthur was simply not being engaged by the regular classroom activities, his teacher had a conference with him about the problem. What was he really interested in? Baseball, of course. So, together, Arthur and the teacher worked out a plan that embraced most areas of the curriculum: He would read and report on a number of adult-level books about baseball, he would write weekly newspaper-style reports of the local college games (which he always attended on weekends), he would develop his math skills by working out a series of higher-level statistics on his favorite players and teams, and he would put together a sketchbook of his portraits of the year's best players.

James, who had nearly been kept back in second grade, started the third grade with a great deal of difficulty. He found even beginning-level exercises in many subjects beyond his grasp. He, too, was soon spending much of his time staring out the window, doodling baseball sketches, and passing notes to friends about baseball games. Clearly, this child, too, had a passionate interest in baseball. James's teacher, too, capitalized on that interest. In conference together, they developed a plan that cut across curriculum areas. James would, with his teacher's help, find books about baseball and other sports that were appropriate for his reading level, he would give oral reports on those books to his friends, he would write paragraphs about his favorite players or most exciting games and read those to his friends, he would work out some basic-level statistics on teams and players, and he would compile a sketchbook of his baseball drawings.

Both of these boys became deeply engaged in their new activities, because those activities dealt directly with their passion for baseball. Where before they were bored or put off by classroom work, they now saw some real-world relevance to what they were doing. And the level of challenge was appropriate for each, stretching their current ability level by gradual degrees.

Limits and Standards

The "dilemma of socialization," the question of whether children can be taught basic behavioral rules without strong extrinsic pressures, is a tough one. Fresh out of college, I started my year as seventh-grade teacher with the attitude that all of the children would hang eagerly on my every word and leap enthusiastically into every project. It never occurred to me that they might have other things on their mind, such as talking and laughing with each other. I learned the hard way about the importance of setting behavioral limits for children. How can this be accomplished in an atmosphere that still supports children's autonomy, intrinsic motivation, individuality, and creativity?

Children should *collaborate* on the "lawmaking" function within the classroom, brainstorming with the teacher on a set of rules that will be necessary for the classroom to work well. After discussion of the rules (and perhaps consequences for rule breaking), they can be written, posted, and signed much like a contract. Students are much more likely to follow rules that they have had a hand in writing, and they are much less likely to feel externally controlled by those rules.

They will also be less likely to feel externally controlled by rules if the rules are presented *informationally*. Children should be given a behavioral constraint along with a good reason for the constraint and an acknowledgment that they might not be enthusiastic about obeying, without a lot of controlling language (such as "This is what I want you to do . . .").

Another area where teachers sometimes feel they must take a "hard line" is in adhering to teaching standards. Especially with the recent popularity of "back to basics" and standard competency exams, teachers have become extremely concerned that students "get it right." In order to preserve creativity in such an atmosphere, it is crucial to make clear the areas in which there are *no* right and wrong answers, the areas where different opinions, different styles, and different approaches can all be equally valid.

Instill Creativity Habits

Teachers have even more opportunities than parents to help children learn creativity skills by modeling those skills. Let your students hear you think aloud as you consider different options for an activity. Try out some new creativity skills, such as looking at problems backward, and lead your students through the thought process with you. If your students consistently hear you say, "Let's find a really creative way of doing this," and "How else can we use this?" and "Let's come up with as many new ideas as possible," they will gradually, habitually adopt a more creative thinking style themselves.

Special Experiences

Children will see that creativity is valued in the classroom if unusual things happen frequently. Here are a few examples of "everyday special experiences" that I have seen teachers use effectively:

Teacher for a Day (or an Hour). This is a partial role-reversal, in which a child takes over as teacher for a time, and the teacher becomes "one of the kids." For example, a child might run the morning calendar routine in kindergarten, with the teacher joining the group to answer questions about what day of the week it is, how many days are left in the month, and how many school days they've had so far in the year. Or, in a higher grade, a child might run a discussion session on a book the class has read or a film they have seen.

Trips. This old favorite can be updated in significant ways to enhance children's creativity. Students should be included in every phase of the trip-planning process, as much as is feasible. They can come up with ideas for fund-raising, if necessary, and actually implement those ideas. Each child can be asked to find something of special interest to him or her on the trip and then research that aspect.

Visitors. Just as parents can stimulate their children's creativity by bringing home interesting and diverse adult visitors, teachers can stimulate their students' creativity by doing the same thing in the classroom. Even teachers who despair of being able to find willing adults who are interesting enough may be surprised if they expand their notions of who might be acceptable. Children can be stimulated by visitors as diverse as the elderly man who carves wooden pipes, or the florist who prepares wedding arrangements, or the homemaker who writes a weekly humor column for the town newspaper. The idea is to expose children to different ways of living and working, different styles of thinking, different modes of expression.

Friday Specials (or any day of the week). The teacher who conceived of this idea initially saw it as a way to "buy" herself individual instruction time with children in the class. In the process, however, she designed a one-hour period each Friday where the entire class had a creativity-enhancing experience. The idea is a simple one: Solicit parent volunteers to come in for one hour on Friday afternoon, three Fridays in a row, and do a creative/fun project with a group of children. Three parents are signed up for each three-week block, so that each parent works with one-third of the children each week. The project or activity is something the parents themselves devise, using their own special talents and interests. While the parents are thus occupying the class, the teacher is free to work individually with different children each week.

Within one half-year period, the Friday Special activities I saw represented a staggering array. They included puppet-making, paper-making, sign language, candy-making, creating a video-taped play, and inventing a word game. For many children, this period became the highlight of the week. The activities stretched their domain skills, engaged their creativity skills, and tapped directly into their intrinsic motivation. They barely realized they were learning so much!

COMBATTING THE CREATIVITY-KILLERS

Even teachers who have prepared a motivating, stimulating classroom must deal with the reality that children come to them already bearing the scars of some potent creativity-killers. There are, however, some concrete ways to combat these forces.

Performance versus Learning

A small group of "gifted" children, ages ten to twelve, had been brought in to take part in a demonstration of teaching high-order cognitive skills. The demonstration was to be led by a university professor, and a large group of teachers from the elementary school had come in to observe. The professor recorded the sobering experience:

The pupils are reserved; there is some evidence of anxiety. My attempts to establish rapport are not very successful.

I offer them a provocative question. "How do you suppose birds learn to fly?"

"What do you mean?" asks Chris.

"I don't understand what you want us to do," says Mark, shifting uncomfortably.

"We didn't study birds yet," says Ann,
explaining the lack of response.
The children are clearly troubled.

These students, like many students at *all* ability levels,
suffer from the "Performance Syndrome." As recently described by an educational researcher, this syndrome is a set
of attitudes that students develop about intelligence, their
own abilities, and their goals in school: *My goal is to have the
teacher say that I did well, and to* not *have the teacher say that I did
poorly. I will always be as smart (or as dumb) as I am today, so I
have to manage things in a way that makes me look as smart as
possible.* Children who suffer from this syndrome work on
tasks only if they are certain they can do well. If they have
low confidence in their abilities on a certain task, they become "helpless"; they avoid challenge, and they give up easily.

The opposite of the Performance Syndrome is the
Learning Orientation. This, too, is a set of attitudes that children have about intelligence, their own abilities, and their
goals in school. But these attitudes differ markedly from
those of the Performance Syndrome. Children who are oriented toward learning seem to believe: *My goal is to learn as
much as I can, to keep doing better. I can become smarter and
smarter by trying new things, so that's what I want to do.* Whether
they have high or low confidence in their ability to do well at
a task, these children will give it a try if they believe they can
learn something. Moreover, they will persist in the face of
difficulty.

Children with the Performance Syndrome will often sac-
rifice learning opportunities for opportunities to look smart.
Ironically, their overconcern with ability may lead them to
shun the very tasks that foster its growth. Moreover, when
they do well on easy tasks, performance-oriented children
tend to feel proud or relieved. In contrast, learning-oriented

children seek out learning opportunities, even if they don't look so smart, and when they do well on easy tasks they tend to feel only bored or disappointed.

Overall, because of the way they feel about themselves and about learning, performance-oriented children are less intrinsically motivated in the classroom, and they will probably be less creative than learning-oriented children.

There are a number of ways that teachers can foster a learning orientation in children. Most importantly, take the focus off "How did you do?" and place it on "What did you learn?" Even very bright students need to be focused on how much they have learned.

Competition

Competition deserves serious attention from teachers because so many parents and school administrators believe that it is desirable, and because it is so firmly entrenched in our culture. Teachers who undertake the noble task of stamping it out of their children have a difficult road ahead.

The most obvious thing you can do about competition is to avoid using it in your own classroom. Beyond that, though, it's necessary to keep children from competing with each other on their own. One positive attack on this problem is to get children working on tasks cooperatively, sharing ideas, and all taking pride in the final product.

Children should understand that people work at different rates on different things, and *that's just as it should be.* They should learn that each person is unique, each has particular strengths and weaknesses. Each child should hear, "If you are trying your best, then you are exactly where you should be in all your subjects. Don't worry about what anyone else is doing, or where anyone else is. Everybody learns in a different way. Trying to learn like someone else is like trying to wear their shoes—there's usually a poor fit!"

The "System"

I can almost hear the teachers out there reading this chapter and saying to themselves: "I could never get away with this stuff in *my* town, not in *this* school system, not with *this* straightjacket of a curriculum!" Most teachers, in most school systems, are required to follow a terribly restrictive curriculum. They are required to give grades on standard report cards. They may even be required to set up the physical classroom in a prescribed fashion. Faced with these daunting obstacles, creative teachers often become discouraged. But it is possible, even within such limitations, to do a great deal in stimulating children's creativity. I have seen it done!

The first line of attack is to test the system. Don't assume constraints that aren't there. Is it impossible to rearrange the classroom into activity centers? Is the week truly so structured that you can't institute Friday Specials? Might it even be possible to send home sets of comments on each student, instead of (or in addition to) grades on report cards? Can you get the students to use self-evaluation instead of relying on your evaluation of them?

Determine where the limits are, then stretch them. If the children don't need twenty-five additional workbook pages drilling them on simple addition, rip those pages out of the workbook. Remember, it is easier to ask forgiveness than to get permission.

Even within fairly restrictive school structures, you can encourage creativity in your classroom by adopting the attitudes and the style I described earlier: Respect children as individuals, show them you find learning important and fun, allow them autonomy within the school day, engage them as active learners, capitalize on their natural interests, show them you value and enjoy creativity. In general, lead them to focus on learning and not on performance.

And don't passively accept things as they are in "the system." Be vocal and forceful, with both educators and parents, about your beliefs in the best way to foster learning, intrinsic motivation, and creativity. Try to become part of the administrative structure, and put your beliefs into practice. In time, it may actually be possible to change the system.

Immunizing Children

As successful as you may be in setting up an atmosphere supportive of intrinsic motivation and creativity, your children will move on; sooner or later, they will end up in a classroom that is not so supportive. Fortunately, there are ways to immunize children against the negative effects of creativity-killing situations.

My colleagues and I devised a set of training sessions in which small groups of children watched videotapes that showed two attractive eleven-year-olds talking with an adult about their schoolwork. We wrote the scripts for the tapes so that this boy and girl would serve as models of intrinsically motivated children who don't let extrinsic constraints overwhelm them. Here is a segment of the script that deals with the issue of having strong, clear intrinsic interests:

Adult: Tommy, of all the things your
teacher gives you to do in school, think
about the one thing you like to do best and
tell me about it.

Tommy: Well, I like social studies the best.
I like learning about how other people live
in different parts of the world. It's also fun
because you get to do lots of projects and
reports. I like doing projects because you
can learn a lot about something on your
own. I work hard on my projects and when

I come up with good ideas, I feel good.
When you are working on something that
you thought of, and that's interesting to
you, it's more fun to do.

Adult: So, one of the reasons you like
social studies so much is because you get to
learn about things on your own. And it
makes you feel good when you do things
for yourself; it makes it more interesting.
That's great!

And here is a script segment designed to teach children
strategies for dealing with extrinsic constraints such as tangible reward:

Adult: It sounds like both of you do the
work in school because you like it, but what
about getting good grades from your
teacher or presents from your parents for
doing well? Do you think about those
things?

Tommy: Well, I like to get good grades,
and when I bring home a good report
card, my parents always give me money.
But that's not what's really important. I
like to learn a lot. There are a lot of things
that interest me, and I want to learn about
them, so I work hard because I enjoy it.

Sarah: Sometimes when I know my
teacher is going to give me a grade on
something I am doing, I think about that.
But then I remember that it's more

important that I like what I'm doing, that I
really enjoy it, and then I don't think about
grades as much.

Adult: That's good. Both of you like to
get good grades, but you both know that
what's really important is how you feel
about your work, and that you enjoy what
you are doing.

A control group of children watched videotapes in
which the adult asked Tommy and Sarah about their favorite
foods, favorite seasons of the year, and so on—nothing to
do with motivation.

In individual sessions a few days later, the children first
filled out a questionnaire measuring motivation, and then
were asked to tell a story. Half of the children worked under
the promise of reward; the other half did not.

The children who had gone through our training scored
higher on intrinsic motivation than children in the control
group. In addition, control-group children told less creative
stories when they were working for reward. By contrast, children in the intrinsic-motivation training group were no less
creative when working for promised reward. In fact, they
were actually more creative!

Parents and teachers needn't produce videotapes to accomplish these goals. You can more simply (and perhaps
more effectively) play out these scenarios yourself and encourage your children to think in these terms. Any genuine
attention to a child's interests should validate and strengthen
them even further.

If children get a steady diet of such immunization treatments, over a long period of time, they will be well equipped
for the maintenance and growth of creativity even in future
hostile environments. Not only will they survive, they will
thrive.

8

GAMES, EXERCISES, DIALOGUES, AND IDEAS: A PRACTICAL GUIDE FOR PARENTS AND TEACHERS

This Card is for
Daddy.
↕
This is your name

urturing a child's creativity is easier said than done. I've made suggestions about general approaches you can take. Here are some concrete ways to do it.

As you read through these examples, take them as just that—examples of the sort of things adults can do to help children grow up creative. Adapt them to your children's level. Use them as springboards for exercising your own creativity in coming up with even better ideas.

CREATING POSITIVE ATTITUDES TOWARD CREATIVITY

Easier and More Fun Than Brushing Your Teeth

Good habits are things you're supposed to do everyday, things that are good for you, and things that don't come naturally—like washing behind your ears, chewing your food twenty times, and brushing your teeth after meals. They're hard to learn, and they're no fun.

But not necessarily. People can develop *creativity habits*—easy to learn and plenty of fun.

It's just past dinnertime at the Greens', and the children are getting ready to pack their own school lunches for tomorrow. In many households, this activity might take fifteen minutes—if the parents could get the children to do it all. But the Greens make a creative event out of even the most ordinary jobs, so lunch-packing sometimes takes half an hour—and the children think it's fun! Tonight, Eleanor is experimenting with the standard peanut butter sandwich by sprinkling raisins and bacon bits inside. Herman likes the idea of the raisins, and adds them to the plastic goody-bag he's making with Cheerios, peanuts, and pumpkin seeds. Julia can't wait to show her friend Sissy the grinning face she cut in the baloney and cheese. And no one can tolerate the idea of a plain brown paper bag. They spend the last five minutes with colored markers and pens, drawing something dazzling that just might brighten things up if tomorrow morning turns out to be a rough one!

The Crazy Great Ideas Bulletin Board

On the first day of school, this classroom looked just like all the others—with one important difference. On the east wall, instead of having some elaborate WELCOME BACK TO SCHOOL sign or autumn scene, the bulletin board was completely empty, right down to the bare corkboard. Above it, in brightly painted letters, was a sign: THE CRAZY GREAT IDEAS BULLETIN BOARD. This, the teacher announced, was the place for everyone in the classroom—including herself—to share great ideas, suggestions, drawings, stories, poems, photographs, and so on—no matter how crazy they might seem. These, she explained, were really the best ideas around, the best new things that they, the classroom members, were doing. The bulletin board, she said, was the place to really show your creativity.

There were only two rules for the board. First, everything placed on the board had to bear the name of the person who put it there, and the date. Second, nothing could be put on the board that was violent, obscene, or mean. Beyond that, anything goes! The teacher explained that, when the

Crazy Great Ideas board was full, she would begin removing the items that had been there the longest and returning them to their owners.

At first, the students were unsure of how to use the board. So, the teacher casually placed a couple of her own items on the board: a striking photo she'd taken of a wild flower, a copy of a suggestion she'd given the principal on how to improve the bus-loading routine at the end of the school day, and a recipe she'd invented for pudding brownies—complete with a bag full of samples for tasting. Before long, the children were bringing in things that they had done: a suggestion for keeping the streets cleaner, some vividly colored cartoons, a poem about a Martian visitor, a self-portrait, a few silly puns, the hand-drawn plans for a model rocket, and several scrambled-word riddles. In the morning, between classes, and during odd free moments, students flocked to the board to check out the latest crazy ideas. People from other classrooms came, too. The teacher and students decided to have weekly discussions of the suggestions and ideas presented on the board. By midyear, the board had become an exciting, active focal point of the class's activities.

STRENGTHENING INTRINSIC MOTIVATION

How Is a Geography Test Fun?

Mother: What are you doing there, Matthew?

Matthew: Aw, I'm studying for a geography test.

Mother: What are you studying?

Matthew: Mr. Hartz says we have to know the capitals of *all* the states by tomorrow. We're going to have a ten-minute quiz. He won't ask us all of them, but we don't know which ones he'll ask.

Mother: Well, how's it going? How do you feel?

Matthew: I hate this. It's going okay, I guess, but I'm really worried about doing well. I hate tests, especially dumb memory tests like this.

Mother: What's *fun* about a geography test?

Matthew: Huh?

Mother: How can a geography test be fun?

Matthew: If it got cancelled.

Mother: (Smiling)   That's not bad! But seriously, think of fun . . .

Matthew: (Laughing)   Think seriously of fun?

Mother: Right. What would make this test fun?

Matthew: If I did well—if I got an A.

Mother: Well, an A is Mr. Hartz's idea of you doing well. What would make *you* feel you'd really done well, really learned this stuff, really beaten this challenge?

Matthew: Well, he's going to ask for thirty capitals. I'd think it was okay if I got twenty-five right, because I have a good memory. But I'd think it was *fantastic* if I got twenty-eight or more right.

Mother: Why not make it a game, then? Why not make that your challenge—to get twenty-five or even twenty-eight! And don't worry about what other kids get, or what grade Mr. Hartz gives you.

Matthew: You mean it?

Mother: Sure . . . the most important thing, really, is what *you're* learning, and how *you* feel about it!

Matthew: (Laughing) Okay, right! And how I feel right now is . . . I don't really hate this so much. Ask me a few of these, will you?

Parents and teachers can use several strategies for maintaining children's intrinsic motivation even in structured testing situations. They can ask children to keep "personal challenge" diaries, where they write down goals for achievement in various areas. (Remember, achievement equals learning and growth, *not* high marks.) Teachers can help children modify their goals over time, so that they are truly challenging for the individual child but not overly difficult. All along, it must be clear that these personal challenges are *not* tied in any way to grades or teacher evaluation.

Another approach is to help the child find some fun in the *content* of the test material. For example, this mother might have asked Matthew what was fun about the states, or state capitals. If he had said, "Just *visiting* them," his mother could have suggested that he imagine he gets to visit every state whose capital he correctly remembers.

The Sky's the Limit

Children will become more aware of their intrinsic interests, and those interests will become stronger, if you ask them questions designed to keep those interests in the forefront.

- What did you enjoy most out of everything you did in school today? Why? Tell me about it.
- What did you like learning the most this year?
- What was the most surprising thing you learned this week? Why did it surprise you?
- What's the thing you're most curious about—the thing you'd most like to learn about?
- What are your favorite books? Why?
- What do you do best? How do you feel about doing that thing?
- Who do you think has the most enjoyable job in the world? Why?
- If you could be an expert in anything at all, what would you be an expert in?
- What things that you do would you really love to do better?
- Who are the five adults you admire the most? Why?
- If you had to do just one thing all day, what would it be?
- If you were going to be stranded on a deserted island for a year, all alone, what would you take with you to keep from being bored (no TV or videos available)?
- What would you do if you could do *anything*?

Reprise: Sculpting the Disney Characters

Recall the scenario from Chapter 5, where a mother and father overplanned a clay-sculpting activity for their children, offered money to the children to get them to do the activity, set up a competition, restricted their choice in what they could sculpt, and gave them rules for neatness in a very controlling manner. Here's a better way in which that scenario could have unfolded:

> *Susan:* What's this stuff in the plastic container?

> *Dad:* Oh, that's a big hunk of modeling clay that Mom and I picked up this morning while we were out doing errands. We thought you kids might enjoy fooling around with it.

> *Sharon:* Hey, this looks like the stuff they had in the art room last year. If you let it harden long enough, you can actually paint your scupltures!

> *Mom:* Right, the woman who runs the art store says you can use most any paint on it after it hardens.

> *Daniel: (Pulling the clay out and plopping it on the table)* Well, can we make some stuff with it now?

> *Dad:* Sure, but just hold on a minute there. First we have to talk about the part that's not much fun—keeping things neat. It's important because the art store woman said this clay will get ruined if it's left exposed to the air too long. Also, this room won't be a good place for anyone to work in if it's a mess. So the clay should be kept in the container, except the pieces you're actually working with, and the table and floor should be protected with these plastic sheets.

Susan: Okay, can we start?

Mom: Sure. Have fun, we'll be in the living room.

Daniel: What should I make?

Mom: Whatever you'd like.

Daniel: But I can't think of anything!

Mom: Well, maybe there's a statue or figurine you like, and you could use that for an idea. Or you can do your favorite animal or a far-out building. Or you can just play around; you don't have to make something that *looks* like something!

Susan: Well, I'm going to do a self-portrait of my head.

Sharon: I'm going to do a self-portrait of my hand!

Daniel: I'm going to see if I can do a Donald Duck like my souvenir from Disney World.

Dad: Terrific ideas! Of course, you can change your ideas around as you go along, too.

Sharon: Is there a prize?

Dad: (Grinning)   Sure there's a prize, but you can *all* win it. It's the fun you're going to have messing around with this stuff!

Now Look at What You've Done!

Children love it when parents show delight in their work by displaying drawings on the refrigerator, saving compositions and stories in a scrapbook, and holding onto treasured handmade crafts no matter how misshapen or useless. These parental attitudes teach children that their work *is* important, that they are doing something "real."

But there is the danger that children will begin to feel they are working only to please the parents. You can avoid this danger by making your children realize they are working to please *themselves*. Put up magnet boards or bulletin boards in your children's rooms, label them "My Favorite Work," and let them have complete control over what gets displayed there. After all, *they* are the ones who will have to look at it all the time! Or purchase a couple of inexpensive picture frames to hang on each child's bedroom wall, the type that have clips at the back so whatever is displayed can be easily changed. Then, encourage your children to think about what they'd like to "show off" to themselves. A parent's pride in a child is wonderful; a child's pride in himself is even better.

What's This Gold Star All About?

Kim had loved school through the first three grades, eager to learn and proud of her own accomplishments. But at the fourth grade level, Kim's school switched from a non-graded "comments" system to a traditional graded system. By the middle of fourth grade, Kim was anxious about school, and nearly frantic about the quarterly grade report. Even though her grades were just fine, she frequently commented to her parents about the children who got a few points higher (or lower) than she. Whenever she brought home a paper with a gold star on it, she immediately tried to translate it into grades: "Two gold stars probably means A, one gold star just means B."

Kim's parents were dismayed by this plunge in her intrinsic motivation, so they set out to do a little "thought reform":

Kim:　Next week is report cards again.

Mother:　Oh? How are you feeling about that?

Kim:　I'm really worried. I hope I didn't go down in math or science, but I think maybe I did. I got one really bad mark in math and two in science this month. I think I'll do well in writing; I hope I'll even get the highest mark in the class!

Father:　What do you think a report card means; what do you think it does?

Kim:　It tells your parents how good you are, how smart you are.

Father:　You know what I think it means?

Kim:　What?

Father:　I think it tells us *and you* how well you did on some tests and some assignments. Not how smart you are, and certainly not how good you are!

Mother:　It's really *your* report card, anyway—not *ours.*

Kim:　What do you mean?

Mother:　It's information for you about how much you know and how hard you tried on some tests and assignments. Actually, I don't think it really tells you too much about what you truly *learned.*

Kim:　Why not?

Mother: Because sometimes kids can do really well on tests just by memorizing, not by really *understanding* the material. And sometimes kids can really learn a lot, but what they learn just doesn't show up on the test!

Father: I'd really be interested in seeing how much *you* think you learned in the things you've been studying. Why not make up your *own* report card, and write down numbers that show how much you think you learned—not what marks you got on tests.

Kim: You mean, like after I get my regular card next week?

Father: Uh-uh. I mean now, before you ever see what marks your teacher puts down. And, by the way, I think the report card *you* fill out is just as "real" as the one you get in school. What you think you learned is just as important as how well the teacher thinks you did.

Mother: Probably *more* important.

Games You Can't Lose

Classroom learning can be made less competitive and—as a result—more creative. A group of researchers have created a cooperative learning paradigm that they call the *jigsaw technique.* The technique was originally designed to decrease interracial prejudice among children, but it can work well with all sorts of groups. In the jigsaw model, children are assigned to work together in small groups. They are given a specific assignment, such as learning about the life of Abraham Lincoln. Each child is given only a piece of the lesson, however. One girl might receive information about Lincoln's birth and early childhood, another girl might get something about his education and adolescence, and a boy in the group might be given material about Lincoln's entry into public life. The children's job is to learn their own piece and then teach it to all the others. In putting together the "information jigsaw puzzle," the children learn the value and technique of cooperation.

Much of the competitiveness in children's lives comes not in regular classroom lessons, but in games. Gradually over time, we should try to replace these competitive activities with cooperative ones: See how well the class, working together, can do at solving a set of "trivia" questions, or let the class work together on creating a mural; have dancers choreograph a number themselves, one in which they all participate; and tell volleyball players that the rules have changed—individual players constantly rotate from one side of the net to the other, and the object is to see how long *everyone* can keep the ball in the air!

Well, I Want to Go to Work Now!

Sandy is always throwing people off balance. Like many mothers, each morning she dresses for the office in relatively traditional clothing, gulps down breakfast, picks up her briefcase, and walks toward the door as the children settle down to breakfast with the baby-sitter. But then Sandy says a most nontraditional thing: "Well, I want to go to work now. See you all later; have a great day!"

The first few times it happened, the baby-sitter thought Sandy was crazy. But then, as now, Sandy's children think that work doesn't have to be a bad thing, that it can be interesting, even fun: intrinsic motivation in the making.

Kill the Judge

Evaluation by other people can undermine intrinsic motivation and creativity, but so can overly harsh *self-evaluation*. Children should learn to not criticize each other, *and* to silence the judge inside themselves from time to time. Everyone should feel free to be curious, to ask questions without feeling stupid. This is how a third-grade teacher I know explained the large sign in her room. KILL THE JUDGE, it said. The sign certainly got her students' attention, and the message stayed with them.

Money Doesn't Have to Change Everything

Father: Hi, Melody, what did you do today?

Melody: I helped Mom with her business.

Father: Really? How—what did you do to help her?

Melody: Well, you know those brochures Mom got printed? The ones with three pages folded in? Well, I helped her by folding up all three hundred of them, putting them in envelopes, then sticking the addresses on. I did a *great* job.

Father: Wow! Was it fun?

Melody: Yes, it was gobs of fun.

Father: Why, Mel?

Melody: For two reasons. First, because it was really a fun job. Second, because I got paid for it!

Father: So it would have been fun even if
you *weren't* paid, but getting paid just made
it nicer?

Melody: Exactly!

The Boy Who Cut the Radio Up

It was thirty years ago, and Jeff—now director of the
Innovation Center for a large organization—was a curious
eight-year-old. He'd found an old, but still working, table
radio in the back corner of a kitchen cabinet. Intent on discovering how it worked, he took it into his father's workshop
one evening, turned it on, removed the back, and proceeded
to snip wires one by one. This was no random destruction,
however. It was *purposeful* destruction, with Jeff taking notes
on which of the radio functions stopped working with each
snip.

Suddenly, his father was at the door. Jeff watched ap-
prehensively as his father slowly walked over, then squatted
down by Jeff's side. "What's this all about?" he asked calmly.
Jeff explained what he'd been trying to do and his father,
genuinely curious, asked Jeff what he'd learned about the
radio's inner workings. Then he pointed out a few more
wires Jeff might want to try, gave him some precautions to
follow, made a few suggestions, and left. No yelling, no punishments, no removal of the radio—just some shared curiosity, a few suggestions, and the freedom to work alone.

BUILDING SKILL WHILE MAINTAINING INTRINSIC MOTIVATION

May I PLEASE Have Piano Lessons?

Lee and Judy had both had discouraging experiences
with piano playing. At the age of eight, Lee had been presented one day with an order from his parents: "We have
bought a piano and you will take lessons. You will learn

something new each week and you will practice each day, and we will get our money's worth by having you entertain on holidays and at dinner parties." Judy had equally little choice. Her older sister had had piano lessons, and there was never any question; starting at age seven, Judy would have them, too. Both Lee and Judy felt quite neutral about the idea at the start but, like so many children, they grew to hate those weekly lessons and the enforced drill. They suffered through for a few years, complaining all the way, until finally their parents let them stop. Now, as adults, Lee and Judy both enjoy music tremendously—and fervently wish that they had learned to play the piano well!

Vowing not to make the same mistakes with their daughter, they hit on a radical idea: Get Becca intrigued with the piano, let her discover the joys of making lovely sounds, and allow her—once she is really "hooked"—to come up with the idea of taking lessons on her own!

So, one Saturday, they invited seven-year-old Becca to come shopping with them. "We thought we'd look at used pianos," they said. "A piano can be a lot of fun to have around the house. Remember Uncle Dave's playing at Grandma's last year, and how great it was to sit around and sing? Well, if *we* have a piano, anybody who comes over can play it."

Becca became very involved in the search for a piano, listening attentively to descriptions of each instrument's special qualities. In the end, she liked the one her parents liked, and became very excited about its arrival. Once it was in the house, Becca could hardly keep her hands off it. Lee and Judy said nothing to try to interest her in the piano; they didn't need to. In fact, playing with the piano became a privilege for Becca, one she had to ask permission to do. Often, during the off-limits "quiet times," she would play on the floor near the piano, eyeing it and the wall clock, waiting for the minute when she could once again pounce on it.

But Becca soon became frustrated with her disorganized

banging on the keyboard. "My songs don't sound like Uncle Dave's songs," she complained. "I want to learn real songs. Please find somebody who can teach me real songs." Eventually, after Becca's pleas convinced Lee and Judy that she was serious, they found someone who could teach her "real songs"—they found her a piano teacher, though a carefully selected one. They interviewed teachers to find one who would work with Becca's high level of interest, who would not place her under great pressure, and who would indeed give her some "real songs" to play right from the very beginning.

Ten years later, Becca is still very happily playing the piano—and very competently, too.

My, How I've Grown!

My friend and colleague, Beth, was a teacher before becoming a psychologist. Each year, when she taught kindergarten, first grade, and second grade, she kept a Personal History folder for each child. As the children progressed through the year, Beth would take samples of their work and file those samples in the Personal History folders. Each folder was unique. For example, one child's folder might include his self-portrait drawn the first week of school, his best math paper, and a paragraph about George Washington that took a particularly long time to write. Another child's folder might include her first attempt at writing a story, the set of beads she made to help herself learn addition, and the collage she made to depict happiness. Both Beth and the child selected objects and papers to go into the folder.

At the end of each school year, Beth would sit down with each child individually and go through the contents of the folder. Almost always, the children would be stunned—and very pleased—by the progress they had made throughout the year. In first grade, for example, from a short, disorganized, and badly spelled story about the bus ride to school, a student might progress to a richly detailed and correctly spelled account of a cross-country airplane trip. Rarely did Beth even need to point out the growth. A child who could not even decipher a little story she wrote so many months earlier would glow with astonished pride at her most recent "publication."

When children can clearly see their own skill growth, a number of good things happen: They are motivated to keep progressing, they feel a sense of *ownership* over their learning process, and they develop a keen and realistic *self*-evaluation system.

The Dangers of Playing It Safe

A friend who is a biologist told me about an interesting experiment: Take a clear glass jar, put ten live flies in it, and put the cap on. In another jar, do the same thing with ten live bees. Lay both jars on their sides with the bottoms facing a source of light, such as the sun. Then remove the caps. If you come back a day later, you will find one empty jar and one jar with ten dead bees. The flies escaped, but the bees could not. It seems that both flies and bees are genetically programmed to fly toward a light source, but the bees are so *tightly* programmed that they really can't do anything else. In the jar, they just kept trying to fly directly toward the light. But because that path was blocked by the glass at the bottom of the jar, they failed. The flies also tried to fly directly toward the light. But, when they ran into the obstacle, they began circling about, exploring their airspace, and eventually turning completely around to find the way out at the open top of the jar.

My friend thinks this is a story about insects, but I think it's a story about creativity and risk taking—a cautionary tale about being too cautious. Like flies, creative people are able to take risks by occasionally doing something that might seem *directly opposite to reaching the goal*. Like bees, overly cautious people are unable or unwilling to try anything but going directly toward the goal in the most obvious way; when they meet an obstacle, they give up or exhaust themselves by trying to push through it. And, in the end, their creativity dies.

Children must, of course, learn rules of physical safety; we don't want them taking risks by going off with strangers or riding their bicycles across the freeway. But they should also learn that taking *some* risks, both physically and intellectually, is the best way for them to grow.

Guess Who's Coming to Dinner?

Saturday, January 17: Our friends Maurice and Amy, who went to China last summer. They'll bring their favorite Szechuan recipe; we'll go to the speciality store and find the ingredients beforehand. Once our guests arrive, we'll all cook together. Maurice will show us some of the special culinary techniques he learned. After dinner, they'll show us the slides they took and tell us about their adventures.

Friday, February 20: The new colleague who moved to the area last fall and his wife. His wife runs a catering business and has promised to bring us copies of her business card, her brochure, and the portfolio of children's and adults' parties that she has put together. She'll also tell us about the evening she catered at the governor's mansion.

Sunday, March 28: Our neighbors, the Rubins, whose son David mows our lawn. David has been learning magic tricks this past year and will share a few of them with us.

Friday, April 3: My graduate student Karl, who served with the Peace Corps in Africa five years ago, and the new day-care teacher, Lori, who just came back from the Peace Corps in Africa. They'll both be bringing their slides to show us, to tell us about their work, the countries they lived in, and the experiences they had.

Friday, May 15: Cheryl, the young artist I met on the plane last week. She'll bring some of the woodcuts she did this spring, and she'll explain the new techniques she invented.

Sunday, June 6: Our friends Kirk and Susan, who have started their own ice cream business. They'll bring a sample for us, and Kirk will also bring along the children's book he just finished writing. We can try out both the ice cream and the story.

Monday, July 13: Mick and Lynda, and their sons, Christopher and Steven, who just returned from a jazz festival. They'll bring recordings of some of the musicians who played there. Christopher will also bring his saxophone, for some live entertainment.

Saturday, August 1: Leslie and her sons, Caleb and Loren. I've asked her to bring the oil painting she just finished of Caleb and Loren at the ocean.

Sunday, September 12: Our friend Rose and her 25-year-old daughter, Barbara, who is both deaf and blind. Barbara just returned from New York University, where she received her college degree Phi Beta Kappa. Through her mother, who will interpret, Barbara will tell us about her college years and her future plans. We've learned the finger alphabet so that we can communicate with Barbara a little ourselves.

Batman in the Classroom

The year I taught seventh grade, I had a particularly difficult time with a group of very bright boys. They were part of the "Advanced Reading and Writing" group that I supervised, and they never wanted to do a thing. That is, they never wanted to do a thing that I suggested—such as reading books from the curriculum list or trying to use the required vocabulary words in essays. Instead, while I went around to work with individual students, they spent their time huddled together reading Batman comics. Batman, it seemed, was their idol. They watched Batman reruns on TV at night and read Batman comics every minute they could steal during the day.

It soon became clear that I was getting nowhere, so I took the old "If you can't beat 'em, join 'em" approach. I met with these boys and asked if they could bring in several of their Batman comics for a new writing project. They looked at me suspiciously, but I assured them that *they* would have control over how the comics were used. The next day, they each showed up with a handful of comic books, eager to see what the crazy teacher had up her sleeve now. I asked them what they liked about the comics, and their answers were enlightening: They loved the action, the strange situations, the weird characters. "Do you think you know those characters pretty well?" I asked. They answered that they knew the characters better than their own brothers and sisters. So I suggested that they write new stories, new adventures, new situations—and that they draw or trace pictures from the comic books so that the stories would actually appear in comic format. "You're kidding," they said. "You want us to sit here for an hour and write comics?"

"Yes," I said, "and write whatever you please—with two stipulations. First, you have to work at least ten of the vocabulary words into each story. Second, your stories have to be fit for public consumption, because they're going on the bulletin board."

That was all it took. For days after that, those boys turned out some of the most creative work I've ever seen. Their stories were outrageous—funny, adventurous, touched with a weird logic. The best part was the actual dialogue. Not only did the boys use the required vocabulary words (correctly), but they raised the level of the characters' vocabularies by making resourceful use of dictionaries and thesauruses. The characters remained delightfully "in character," but their utterances had improved by about six grade levels. Soon children from all over the school were coming into our room to read the latest bulletin board comics. But no one enjoyed them more than the young authors, who would stand there reading their work over and over again.

The Opposites Game

My friend Diane used to work as a children's entertainer for the city parks each summer when she was in high school —a job that gave her ample opportunity to use her own creativity. One game she devised is especially good for teaching children a most important creativity skill: *There is often no such thing as a right answer.*

It's called the Opposites Game. The rules are simple: Player 1 says a word, and Player 2 gives the opposite of that word. Then Player 2 says a word, and Player 1 gives the opposite. During the warm-up period of the game, especially with young children, it's best to start with words that have simple opposites. But the game really becomes interesting— and creative—when the words become more complex, when they don't have clear opposites. Often, the players will discuss different possible answers, explaining one or the other, and mulling over which answer might be "better" than another. The game can be expanded to include several players and it can, of course, be played without an adult.

Here's an example of how the Opposites Game might go:

Adult: What's the opposite of OUT?

Child: IN! Now, what's the opposite of GO?

Adult: COME. What's the opposite of HERE?

Child: THERE. What's the opposite of HAPPY?

Adult: SAD. And . . . what's the opposite of FRUSTRATED?

Child: Hmmm . . . CALM?

Adult: Yeah, I think calm is pretty good. Any other ideas?

Child: How about . . . the opposite of FRUSTRATED is SATISFIED?

Adult: Great! That sounds really good.

Child: What's the opposite of GRANDDAUGHTER?

Adult: Hmmm . . . How about GRANDMOTHER?

Child: I was thinking of GRANDSON. Because granddaughter is a girl, and grandson is a boy. But grandmother could be a good opposite, too, because . . . one is young and the other is old.

Adult: Yes! Now, what's the opposite of FLOWER?

Child: FLOWER? Mmmm, that's a tough one. Maybe SEED? Because a flower is all grown, and a seed isn't grown at all?

Adult: That's interesting. I really like that one! Any others for FLOWER?

Child: Yes. ROCK! It's not living at all, and a flower is living. What's *your* opposite for flower?

Adult: I don't know . . . Seed and rock both make a lot of sense. But your idea for rock gave *me* an idea. How about DROUGHT—because a drought can *kill* a flower!

Child: Hey, yeah! Now, here's a toughie. What's the opposite of OUTER SPACE?

Trading Places

Christene is going to be me on Halloween, and I am going to be her. It was her idea, but I'm going along with it. I know it will help her (and me) learn the creativity skill of taking new perspectives. The main reason, though, is that I think it'll be a lot of fun.

Halloween will be on a Saturday so, from the time we wake up, she'll be the mom and I'll be the kid. She'll be in charge of supervising cooking and chores, while I'll get to watch a few cartoons on TV. I'll have to feed the cat and clean the litter box, but she'll do the laundry. She'll probably make a few long-distance calls to relatives while I play with my calculator or paint a picture. Then she might write a few pages on the word processor; I'll be busy playing dress-up with a few of her old clothes. We'll walk down to the store so that she can choose and buy the Halloween candy. I'll beg her to buy a few extra treats for me, but she'll probably refuse.

The evening will be the most fun. For trick-or-treat, she'll dress up in one of my business suits, pull her hair back at the neck into a no-nonsense style, put on a bit of makeup, and take my shoulder strap briefcase for stashing candy. I'll follow along behind in some jeans, sneakers, an extra-large sweatshirt, and an extra-extra-large vest. I'll put my hair in a ragged ponytail and sling a pink backpack over my shoulder. As she rings each doorbell, Christene will pull out one of my old business cards to hand to the lady (or man) of the house. On the back, she will have printed TRICK OR TREAT!

So don't be alarmed if you open the door on Halloween to see a very little professional woman with a very big girl lurking in the background.

Next year she wants to trade places with her cat.

CREATIVE FUN

Not Sold in Any Store

In one of the most creative families I know, the parents have a real aversion to store-bought gifts. They prefer to give activities or events (such as outings and trips), personal favors (such as baby-sitting certificates to their housebound friends), or handmade crafts. If they do buy a ready-made greeting card, they get a blank one so they can add their own message or verse.

Samantha has picked up this attitude from her parents; the gifts she gives family and friends are remarkable. Last Christmas, for example, she gave: a gift certificate for ten car washings to her father, a hand-embroidered belt to her mother, a poem she'd written called "Grandma's Hands" to her grandmother, and a gift certificate to her younger brother promising to play "Stratego" with him twenty times without complaining.

Music Painting

The children sat at their desks armed with their favorite drawing and coloring materials (what their teacher Miss Cooper playfully calls implements of construction—paper, markers, pencils, pens, crayons, paints. "You'll hear some music that was written by Mozart," she said. "It might be familiar to some of you. But it doesn't matter whether you've heard it before." What you're going to do is *paint* the music, *draw* the music, *color* the music."

"But what should we draw?" they asked. "What do you want it to look like?"

"I don't know what it *should* look like. It should only look like the music *sounds* to you . . . however the music makes you *feel.* Draw that feeling. It doesn't have to look like a picture or anything; it can just be colors and shapes, if that's what you want."

Softly, the music began. The children sat frozen, somewhat befuddled. But there at her desk was Miss Cooper, swaying her head to the music and busily drawing something on her sketch pad. Soon the children started in, at first hesitantly, looking at each other's papers, but then confidently, absorbed only in what they were doing. Many of them seemed startled five minutes later when Miss Cooper stopped the music.

"Now get a clean sheet of paper and we'll do another one. The music is by the same composer, Mozart, but I think it might sound very different to you. Just put on the paper anything that comes to mind as you listen to the music."

After the second piece had stopped, they talked about how the music "felt" to them. Most of them agreed that the first piece felt sad, somber, slow, strict. The second piece was fast and energetic, talkative or maybe angry. They were amazed at how similar their feelings were, and even more amazed when they shared their drawings. Although no two papers were alike, nearly all of the children (and Miss Cooper too) had chosen cool colors for the first one, and had used curling, sloping, gentle shapes. On the second paper, though, the colors were hot and bold, the lines sharp, the contrasts strong.

Many parents were baffled when the children brought home these striking papers and referred to them as "Music Paintings." But the *children* knew what they meant.

The Mystery Weekend

Imagine how your children would react if you told them that next weekend, the family was taking off in the car on a mystery adventure. What's the mystery? No one knows exactly where you're going or what you're going to do.

Each person in the family gets maps and booklets to study for a few days before the weekend, because each is responsible for thinking up "Top-Secret Destinations." A Top-Secret Destination is an idea for a place to visit or a thing to do within the projected driving area for each day (say, one hundred miles). Because no one knows in advance which *direction* the family will be headed, each person must come up with possible destinations in each direction. But these must be kept top secret, with each person guarding his own ideas and plans until they are needed.

If it will be an overnight mystery trip, each family member must pack a Versatile Suitcase. This is a suitcase that includes clothing specified by each family member. For example, Mother might say that her destinations will require bathing suits and raincoats. Father's might require warm jackets and hiking shoes, while Alice's require formal attire.

Besides the maps, guidebooks, and suitcases, all that you need to play this game is some imagination and four slips of paper on which the words *north, south, east,* and *west* are printed. When the mystery trip begins, the family gets into the car, and someone picks one of the four slips out of a hat (without looking). The family must head in whichever direction is chosen.

Then the people who have planned destinations in that direction negotiate with each other by saying how long it will take to get to their destination and, perhaps, dropping hints about what the destination involves. The trick is to direct the driver as close as possible to the chosen site without giving away the Top-Secret Destination—until the last minute.

After the family has enjoyed whatever activity lay in store at that site, they draw again from the hat, and head out in whatever direction is chosen next. If the group passes something that looks interesting, it's not against the rules to stop —even if it wasn't in anyone's secret plans!

Flexibility, adaptability, humor, patience, and cunning are the keys to this game. Each family will want to devise its own set of rules for the Mystery Weekend, and some may want to make it a Mystery Day or even a Mystery Week. The main point is to have fun working creatively together and surprising each other.

The Waiting Game

Beth is now a very creative adolescent, one who writes lovely short stories and takes grinning self-portraits with her camera *(Mona Lisa with Braces)*. I can't help but think that a lot of that creativity came from the fun she had with her mother in restaurants over the years.

Think of all the time that gets wasted while parents and children wait in restaurants. They wait to get their names taken, wait to get seated, wait for a waitress, and wait for the food. At best, the time is usually spent in resigned silence. At worst, it's a battle between a cranky child and an often crankier adult.

But Beth's mom always carried a small blank pad in her purse, a colored pen or two, and lots of creative imagination. Sometimes Beth would draw, scribble, or try out letters when she was first learning the alphabet. Other times, her mom would draw riddles on the page for Beth to solve: In the first column, pictures of a hat, a man, and a clock; in the second column, the letters C, H, and M. Beth's challenge was to match pictures and letters. They would try to tell a story with nothing but pictures, or send each other notes. Beth would play waitress sometimes, taking her mom's order (and the order of any friendly people at adjoining tables). They would carefully watch other people in the restaurant and make up elaborate stories about their lives and their futures. They would imagine they'd just come from another planet, or just awakened after being asleep for ten years; how strange everything looked and sounded! They would pretend they couldn't speak each other's language, and would try to communicate through gestures, facial expressions, and pantomime. They would practice the finger alphabet, which they'd copied from a book. They would mouth sentences and try to read each other's lips. Almost invariably, Beth would be terribly disappointed when the food finally came and she actually had to eat.

Creative Parties

Somewhere around the end of March each year, Christene and I—along with most of the Boston population—are fed up with winter. We're tired of the colorless woods behind our house, and we're tired of the relentless cold. So we banish winter for a night, just when we think we can't stand it another minute. We call a couple of friends and invite them to come to Tahiti with us, right in our own home. The only requirement is that they must wear (or bring) summer clothing—shorts, sundresses, and so on.

Here's how we create summertime in our home. First, we turn up the thermostat to 85°; we don't just want the house to feel warm, we want it to feel hot. We build a gigantic fire in the fireplace to warm up the living room even further. Using a blue sheet for the ocean and a brown sheet for the sand, Christene creates a beach on the living room rug. She even takes out her box of seashells and scatters them along the "shore." By this time, I've usually managed to get a large chicken roasting on the barbecue kettle outside. (Roasting time must be increased by some factor relating to the wind chill outdoors!) Before changing into our sundresses, we complete the party setting in the living room: a bunch of exotic tropical flowers in a vase on the mantel, a few beach towels laid out for the picnic, and the beach umbrella perched in its weighted stand.

Our activities all evening liberate us from winter's grasp. We run around the house barefoot, we eat barbecued chicken, potato salad, corn on the cob, and popsicles, we drink iced tea, we listen to Beach Boys albums during the meal, we have a seashell hunt (similar to an Easter Egg hunt, only cleaner), we watch a summertime video movie and we even—after the guests have left—put on our bathing suits and go for a nice warm dip in the bathtub.

When spring does finally arrive, we have our annual Petunia Patch party. The name of the party, and the idea for it, came from my pet nickname for Christene. Since the day she was born, I've been calling her Petunia Patch; it just seemed to suit her. So, a few years ago, when we decided to finally put some flowers in our front yard, we instituted the Petunia Patch party. The idea is an expansion of Huck Finn's brainstorm—you get friends to do your work for you (or at least *with* you), and make them think it's fun! We invite an assortment of adults and children—Christene's friends, their siblings and parents, my friends, interesting acquaintances we've made. We ask each person to bring a few petunias, in any color and type they wish. As guests arrive, they help themselves to the snacks and drinks we've laid out and—in a somewhat disorganized fashion—help to prepare the flower bed. We rake, pick out last year's wood chips, add fertilizer, smooth the soil. Then, after everyone has arrived, we set the petunias out on top of the soil, rearranging them, making group decisions about the most pleasing arrangement. Christene has the honor of planting the first flower, after which everyone digs in, as it were. We then spread out the bark chips, water the petunias, and arrange ourselves around the flower bed for a group photo (which I will eventually send out to everyone who attended). The party ends with a long, lazy barbecue supper.

Parties, which have become a commonplace feature of most children's lives, provide a great opportunity for creative fun. They give adults and children the chance to live out their fantasies, to break away from routines, to realize they can think of wonderful new ways to do the same old everyday things.

Some other creative parties:

The "Test-It-Out" Birthday Party. This is the child's version of *Consumer Reports.* The parents assembled several different versions of the same toy product—in this case, they bought or made a number of different bubble pipes for blowing soap bubbles. When the children arrived, they each got a colorful paper smock apron with their name and the birthday boy's name printed on it. (This smock served two purposes; it kept the children's clothes clean while they were playing with the bubble pipes, and it gave them a party souvenir which could be signed by all the other children.) The party activity (conducted in the backyard) consisted of each child trying out each bubble pipe and filling in a rating sheet on how much fun it was, how well it worked, how pretty the bubbles were, and so on. Afterward, while the children were having refreshments, one of the parents tallied up the results and announced them. The bubble pipes were then raffled off as party favors.

The Dramatic Halloween Party. At this party, the children created a scary audio play. The parent provided a sketchy story on the order of "It was a dark and stormy night . . . " and plenty of sound effect materials: big shoes for stomping on the floor, paper to crinkle, a bell, sandpaper, and so on. The children, as a group, expanded on the story, making changes in the narrative. The adult supervised only to make sure that each child had at least one sound effects "part" in the play (the howling wind, the cackling witches, the thudding footsteps). After the script was finalized and rehearsed, the tape recorder was turned on to record the final performance. At the end, the narrator gave the name of each child and his or her particular sound effect. The result wasn't exactly "War of the Worlds," but it was so delightful that the children begged to hear it at least six times before the party was over.

Christmas in Other Lands. This is an extended-family party, where each year the child cousins select a country that celebrates Christmas in a different way, research the customs and activities, and then—with the grown-ups' help—re-create as much of that foreign Christmas as they can.

Reunions. Why should people have to wait twenty-five years to be reunited with school chums? A friend of mine wondered the same thing when his child complained of missing the kids she'd been with in first grade the previous year. (They live in a school system where class lists are made randomly. So in the second-grade classroom, a child might know only three or four children who were also grouped with her in the first grade.) Together, this parent and child planned a "First-Grade Reunion," to be held early in the second-grade year. They even put goodies for each child in a folder that was the same color as his or her first-grade "work folder."

One Hundred Thousand Miles. The car almost seemed like a member of the family, it had been with us so long: Ten years and 99,992 miles. We were so excited about seeing the numbers change to 00000 at 100,000 miles that we baked a cake, got some hats and noisemakers, picked up a few friends, and drove around until we hit the magic point on the odometer. At exactly 100,000 miles, we pulled into a vacant parking lot, sounded the horn, made a racket with the noisemakers, lit candles, cut the cake, and had a party. The adults enjoyed it at least as much as the kids.

A TEST FOR CREATIVE CHILDHOOD ENVIRONMENTS

Here is a test I have devised to help you determine how well your home environment or school environment is supporting your children's intrinsic motivation and creativity. You can answer the items yourself, thinking truthfully about the home or school environment, listening carefully to the remarks your children make, and answering the items as you think the children would. Or, the children can answer the items themselves—as long as they understand that there are no "right" or "wrong" answers!

All of the items are True-False. At the end of the test, I've presented the responses that indicate a creativity-supporting environment. If most of your answers (or your child's answers) agree with the responses I've indicated, the environment is probably supporting creativity. Answers that differ from mine indicate possible areas for improving the environment.

I've written the items to refer to the *home environment*. They can easily be adapted for the *school environment*.

Instructions: Answer each question by saying how you usually feel *at home*. There are no right or wrong answers.

_____ 1.   I can ask questions here at home without worrying about sounding dumb.

_____ 2.   I have a lot of choices about how to get something done.

_____ 3.   I usually know what I'm going to get if I do something well.

_____ 4.   There are a lot of rules here at home.

_____ 5.   I am usually asked what *I* think about things.

_____ 6.   Things don't change much around here.

_____ 7. I have to get permission before trying anything new.

_____ 8. My parents really care about what I have to say.

_____ 9. The most important thing here at home is being the best.

_____10. My parents encourage me to be creative.

_____11. I am usually told how to do things.

_____12. My parents are usually watching what I do and how I do it.

_____13. My parents encourage me to figure things out for myself.

_____14. There is a lot of competition here at home.

_____15. I have a lot of say in what I'm going to do at home.

_____16. I know the reasons behind most of the rules we have at home.

_____17. I'm allowed to please myself in what I do.

_____18. My ideas are included in important decisions at home.

_____19. My parents use bribes to get me to do what they want.

_____20. My parents like to do things creatively.

_____21. I get punished for making mistakes at home.

_____22. My parents really enjoy what they do.

_____23. My parents are patient with me.

_____24. You have to be really quiet here at home.

_____25. My parents encourage me to think of new ways for doing things.

_____26. Work is fun here at home.

_____27. I do the things I do mostly to please my parents.

_____28. I get to meet a lot of different, interesting adults at home.

_____29. My parents are ashamed of me.

_____30. My parents really like me to ask a lot of questions.

_____31. I am under a lot of pressure to do good work.

_____32. Keeping things neat is one of the most important rules at home.

_____33. I have a lot of freedom in what I do at home.

_____34. My parents really like me.

_____35. It's very important to my parents that I get a good report card.

_____36. There's a lot of joking and laughing here at home.

_____37. My parents respect me.

_____38. It's okay for me to tell my parents how I feel.

_____39. My parents try to find out what I'm interested in.

_____40. My parents are always trying something new.

_____41. I've been taught that my parents are always right.

_____42. There are a lot of interesting things to look at here at home.

_____43. My parents usually have every detail of a job or activity planned out for me.

_____44. I feel special at home.

_____45. My parents are always suggesting new activities.

_____46. I have a lot of freedom to "do my own thing" at home.

_____47. The major reason I do my work at home is to get treats, prizes, or money.

_____48. My parents encourage me to use my imagination when I'm playing alone or with friends.

_____49. I get criticized a lot at home.

_____50. My parents like spending time with me.

Responses that indicate a creativity-supporting environment:

1. T	2. T	3. F	4. F	5. T	6. F
7. F	8. T	9. F	10. T	11. F	12. F
13. T	14. F	15. T	16. T	17. T	18. T
19. F	20. T	21. F	22. T	23. T	24. F
25. T	26. T	27. F	28. T	29. F	30. T
31. F	32. F	33. T	34. T	35. F	36. T
37. T	38. T	39. T	40. T	41. F	42. T
43. F	44. T	45. T	46. T	47. F	48. T
49. F	50. T				

In your effort to help your children grow up creative, you are giving them a precious, lifelong gift. I wish you (and them) a most creative future!

SUGGESTED READINGS

Books about the Nature of Creativity

Amabile, T. M. 1983. *The social psychology of creativity.* New York: Springer-Verlag.
A more detailed and technical description of much of the creativity theory and research described in this book.

Campbell, D. 1977. *Take the road to creativity and get off your dead end.* Allen, TX: Argus Communications. (Available through the Center for Creative Leadership, Greensboro, NC, [919-288-7210].)
A brief and highly readable introduction to the basics in the psychology of creativity.

Gardner, H. 1982. *Art, mind, and brain: A cognitive approach to creativity.* New York: Basic Books.
A detailed examination of the mental processes involved in creativity.

Perkins, D. N. 1981. *The mind's best work.* Cambridge, MA: Harvard University Press.
A scholarly yet readable exploration of the creative process in the arts, sciences, and everyday life.

Wallach, M. and Kogan, N. 1965. *Modes of thinking in young children.* New York: Holt, Reinhart and Winston.
A description of research into the relationship between children's IQ and creativity.

General Books for Stimulating Creativity

Burns, M. 1976. *The book of think.* Boston: Yolla Bolly Press.
Tricks for thinking up new ideas, even when you are puzzled and perplexed.

Fluegelman, A. 1976. *The new games book.* Garden City, NY: Doubleday.

A collection of games for all ages where there are no spectators and no losers; rather, there is room for creativity by changing rules and altering goals.

Guilford, J. P. 1977. *Way beyond the IQ: Guide to improving intelligence and creativity.* Buffalo, NY: Creative Education Foundation and Creative Synergetic Associates.

Leff, H. L. 1984. *Playful perception.* Burlington, VT: Waterfront Books.
A collection of dozens of exercises that can be used by both children and adults to perceive the world more creatively.

MacKinnon, D. W. 1978. *In search of human effectiveness: Identifying and developing creativity.* Buffalo, NY: Creative Education Foundation and Creative Synergetic Associates.

Parnes, S. J., Noller, R. B., and Biondi, A. M. 1977. *Guide to creative action.* New York: Charles Scribner's Sons.

Schneider, T. 1976. *Everybody's a winner.* Boston: Yolla Bolly Press.
Delightful descriptions of new games and new ways to play old ones, along with new ways to think about winning and losing; a great curative for competition fever.

Stein, M. I. 1974, 1975. *Stimulating creativity: Volume I and Volume II.* New York: Academic Press.

Books for Stimulating Children's Creativity

Benjamin, C. L. 1985. *Writing for kids.* New York: Harper & Row.
A guidebook for children ages eight to twelve who want to write creatively; suggestions for coming up with ideas, illustrating sentences, starting a writer's notebook, and writing books.

Khatena, J. 1978. *The creatively gifted child: Suggestions for parents and teachers.* New York: Vantage Press.

Profiles in science for young people. 1987. Hauppauge, NY: Baron's Educational Series.
A series for older children (around ages eleven to thirteen) consisting of inspiring biographies of accomplished inventors and scientists; includes profiles on Einstein (R. Cwiklik), Curie (A. E. Steinke), Darwin (R. Skelton), and Edison (L. Egan).

Renzulli, J. 1976. *New directions in creativity.* New York: Harper & Row.

Stein, S. B. 1975. *The kids' kitchen takeover.* New York: Workman.
A collection of extremely creative ideas for children's kitchen projects (edible and nonedible ones), including "ooblech," "how to get a cork out of a bottle without touching it ," "gelatin glop," fish prints, noodle sculpture, and "start your own bread business."

Taylor, B. 1987. *Weekly Reader presents: Be an inventor.* New York: Field Publications.
Profiles of school children who have entered their ideas in the Weekly Reader's National Invention Contest; presents would-be inventors with an entertaining guide to thinking creatively.

Torrance, E. P. 1962. *Guiding creative talent.* Englewood Cliffs, NJ: Prentice-Hall.

Treffinger, D. J. 1980. *Encouraging creative learning for the gifted and talented: A handbook of methods and techniques.* Ventura, CA: Ventura County Superintendent of Schools Office.

NOTES

PREFACE

Page ix:
 Quote from Pablo Casals.
 A.E. Kahn, 1970, *Joys and sorrows: Reflections by Casals* (New York: Simon and Schuster), 295.

Chapter 1

Page 3:
 Quote from Carl Sagan.
 C. Sagan, "Why we must continue to be explorers," *Parade Magazine* (November 22, 1987), 5.

Page 5:
 Creativity and psychological health.
 F. Barron, 1968, *Creativity and personal freedom* (Princeton, NJ: Van Nostrand).
 and
 L. S. Kubie, 1961, *Neurotic distortion of the creative process* (New York: Noonday Press).

Pages 6–8:
 Quotes from Pablo Casals.
 A. E. Kahn, 1970, *Joys and sorrows: Reflections by Pablo Casals* (New York: Simon and Schuster), 37, 36, 26, 30 & 35.

Chapter 2

Pages 21–22:
 Gifted California schoolchildren.
 L. M. Terman, 1954, "The discovery and encouragement of exceptional talent," *American Psychologist 9*, 221–30.

Page 21:
 Intelligence and creativity in children.
 J. Getzels and P. Jackson, 1962, *Creativity and intelligence: Explorations with gifted students* (New York: Wiley).
 and

M. Wallach and N. Kogan, 1965, *Modes of thinking in young children* (New York: Holt, Rinehart and Winston).

Page 22:

Creative writers and depression.

N.J.C. Andreasen and A. Canter, 1974, "The creative writer: Psychiatric symptoms and family history," *Comprehensive Psychiatry 15;* 123–31.

Page 33:

Trevor Ferrell story.

W. Plummer, "Philadelphia's street people have found a ministering angel in tiny Trevor Ferrell," *People* (March 26, 1984), 60–62.

Chapter 3

Page 37:

Quote from Einstein.

B. Hoffmann and H. Dukas, 1972, *Albert Einstein: Creator and rebel* (New York: Viking Press), 7.

Page 41:

The problem-presentation stage of creativity.

J. W. Getzels and M. Csikszentmihalyi, 1976, *The creative vision: A longitudinal study of problem-finding in art* (New York: Wiley-Interscience).

Page 43:

Research on children's abilities in different domains.

H. Gardner, 1983, *Frames of mind* (New York: Basic Books).

Page 44:

Quote about Mozart from Johann Schachtner.

P. Woodford, 1977, *Mozart: His life and times* (Kent, UK: Midas Books), 19.

Chapter 4

Page 53:

Quote from André Gide.

A. Gide, 1949, *The fruits of the earth,* trans. D. Bussy (New York: Knopf), 33.

Page 53:

Quote from Robert Oppenheimer letter.

J. Bernstein, 1987, "The life it brings—I," *The New Yorker* (January 26, 1987), 35.

Page 55:
Research on children's mastery.
S. Harter, 1978, "Effectance motivation reconsidered: Toward a developmental model," *Human Development 21*, 34–64.

Page 55:
Self-determination as part of intrinsic motivation.
E. L. Deci and R. M. Ryan, 1985, *Intrinsic motivation and self-determination in human behavior* (New York: Plenum Press).

Page 55:
Soma puzzle studies.
M. Zuckerman et al., 1978, "On the importance of self-determination for intrinsically motivated behavior," *Personality and Social Psychology Bulletin 4*, 443–46.

Page 57:
Quote from Arthur Schawlow.
"Going for the gaps," Interview in *The Stanford Magazine* (Fall 1982), 42.

Page 58:
Study of choice in collage materials.
T. M. Amabile and J. Gitomer, 1984, "Children's artistic creativity: Effects of choice in task materials," *Personality and Social Psychology Bulletin 10*, 209–15.

Page 59:
Study of creative writers.
T.M. Amabile, 1985, "Motivation and creativity: Effects of motivational orientation on creative writers," *Journal of Personality and Social Psychology 48*, 393–99.

Chapter 5

Page 71:
Quote from Einstein.
A. Einstein, 1949, Autobiography. In P. Schilpp, *Albert Einstein: Philosopher-scientist* (Evanston, IL: Library of Living Philosophers), 19.

Pages 72, 73:
Quote from Sylvia Plath.
T. Hughes and F. McCullough, eds., 1982, *The Journals of Sylvia Plath* (New York: Dial), 305.

Page 72:
Evaluation of children's spin-painting.
S. Berglas, T. M. Amabile and M. Handel, "An examination of the effects of verbal reinforcement on creativity" (Paper presented at the meeting of the American Psychological Association, New York, September 1979).

Page 72:
Evaluation effects on adult creativity.
T. M. Amabile, 1979, "Effects of external evaluation on artistic creativity," *Journal of Personality and Social Psychology* *37*, 221–33.

and

T. M. Amabile, P. Goldfarb, and S.C. Brackfield, 1982, "Effects of social facilitation and evaluation on creativity" (Unpublished manuscript, Brandeis University, Waltham, MA).

Page 73:
"Hidden costs" in rewards.
M. R. Lepper and D. Greene, eds., 1978, *The hidden costs of reward* (Hillsdale, NJ: Erlbaum).

Page 73:
Quote from T. S. Eliot.
E. Simpson, 1982, "Eliot and friends." *New York Times Book Review* (January 24, 1982), 11.

Page 73:
Quote from Dostoevsky.
W. Allen, 1948, *Writers on writing* (London: Phoenix House), 231.

Page 74:
Straightforward tasks versus complex tasks: reward effects.
K. O. McGraw, 1978, "The detrimental effects of reward on performance: A literature review and a prediction model," In M. R. Lepper and D. Greene, eds., *The hidden costs of reward* (Hillsdale, NJ: Erlbaum).

Page 74:
Candle and thumbtacks study.
S. Glucksberg, 1962, "The influence of strength of drive on functional fixedness and perceptual recognition," *Journal of Experimental Psychology* *63*, 36–41.

Page 75:
Effects of reward on children's creativity.
T. M. Amabile, B. A. Hennessey, and B. S. Grossman, 1986, "Social influences on creativity: The effects of contracted-for reward," *Journal of Personality and Social Psychology 50,* 14–23.
Page 75:
Effects of reward on high school students' creativity.
A.W. Kruglanski, I. Friedman, and G. Zeevi, 1971, "The effects of extrinsic incentive on some qualitative aspects of task performance," *Journal of Personality 39,* 606–17.
Page 75:
Quote from Sylvia Plath.
T. Hughes and F. McCullough, eds., 1982, *The journals of Sylvia Plath* (New York: Dial), 304.
Page 76:
Effects of competition on children's creativity.
T. M. Amabile, 1982, "Children's artistic creativity: Detrimental effects of competition in a field setting," *Personality and Social Psychology Bulletin 8,* 573–78.
Page 78:
Quote from Einstein.
A. Einstein, 1949, Autobiography. In P. Schlipp, *Albert Einstein: Philosopher-scientist* (Evanston, IL: Library of Living Philosophers), 18.
Pages 79, 80:
Limit-setting study.
R. Koestner et al., 1984, "Setting limits on children's behavior: The differential effects of controlling vs. informational styles on intrinsic motivation and creativity," *Journal of Personality 52,* 233–48.
Page 87:
Teachers' attitudes toward control.
E. L. Deci et al., 1981, "An instrument to assess adults' orientations toward control versus autonomy with children: Reflections on intrinsic motivation and perceived competence," *Journal of Educational Psychology 73,* 642–50.
Page 87:
"Pygmalion" study of intellectual gains in children.
R. Rosenthal and L. Jacobson, 1966, "Teachers' expectan-

cies: Determinants of pupils' IQ gains," *Psychological Reports 19*, 115–18.

Page 87:
"Pygmalion" study of creativity gains in children.
R. Rosenthal, S. S. Baratz, and C. M. Hall, 1974, "Teacher behavior, teacher expectations, and gains in pupils' rated creativity," *The Journal of Genetic Psychology 124*, 115–21.
Page 88:
Children's attributions for failure.
C. I. Diener and C. S. Dweck, 1978, "An analysis of learned helplessness: Continuous changes in performance, strategy, and achievement cognitions following failure," *Journal of Personality and Social Psychology 36*, 451–62.
Page 89:
The "fourth-grade slump" in creativity.
E. P. Torrance, 1974, *Norms technical manual: Torrance test of creative thinking* (Bensenville, IL: Scholastic Testing Service).
Pages 90, 91:
Quotes from Ansel Adams.
A. Adams, 1985, *Ansel Adams: An autobiography* (Boston: Little, Brown and Company), 17 and 21.

Chapter 6

Page 103:
Freedom-granting parents (and other parent attitudes).
D. W. MacKinnon, 1978, *In search of human effectiveness* (New York: Creative Synergetic Associates).
Page 104:
Comparison of "creative" and "less creative" homes.
J. S. Dacey, 1987, "Discriminating characteristics of the families of highly creative adolescents" (Unpublished manuscript, Center for Research on Creativity, Lexington, MA).
Page 105:
Parents' attitudes about themselves.
B. C. Miller and D. Gerard, 1979, "Family influences on the development of creativity in children: An integrative review," *The Family Coordinator 28*, 295–312.

Page 107:
Quotes from Steven Spielberg's mother.
F. A. Bernstein, 1986, "Present at the creation," *People* (May 5, 1986), 95–99. (Excerpted from F.A. Bernstein, *The Jewish Mother's Hall of Fame*)
Page 108:
Moving frequently.
D. W. MacKinnon, 1978, *In search of human effectiveness* (New York: Creative Synergetic Associates).
Page 109:
Features of creative homes.
J. S. Dacey, 1987, "Discriminating characteristics of the families of highly creative adolescents" (Unpublished manuscript, Center for Research on Creativity, Lexington, MA), 6.
Page 110:
Quote from letter to Linda Ellerbee.
L. Ellerbee, 1986, *And so it goes: Adventures in television* (New York: G.P. Putnam's Sons), 254.
Page 111:
Quotes from Margaret Mead.
M. Mead, 1972, *Blackberry Winter: My earlier years* (New York: William Morrow and Co.), 53–54 & 72.
Page 112:
Research on creative models.
D. W. MacKinnon, 1978, *In search of human effectiveness* (New York: Creative Synergetic Association).

and

D. K. Simonton, 1984, *Genius, creativity, and leadership* (Cambridge, MA: Harvard University Press).
Page 116:
Quotes from Seth Green's mother.
J. Logan, "Precocious child on a mission," *Boston Globe*, February 8, 1987, A15 & A18.
Page 116:
Quote from Einstein's father.
B. Hoffmann and H. Dukas, 1972, *Albert Einstein: Creator and rebel* (New York: Viking Press), 33.

Page 117:
Quote from John Updike.
J. Updike, "Rapt by the radio," *Boston Globe, Literati on the Red Sox,* October 6, 1986.

Page 117:
Quote from Eudora Welty.
G. Caldwell, "Eudora Welty," *Boston Globe,* October 2, 1986, 76.

Page 118:
Quote from Richard Feynman.
S. S. Schweber, 1986, "Feynman and the visualization of space-time processes," *Review of Modern Physics 58,* 449–508. Quote on 451.

Pages 118–119:
Quote from Robert Oppenheimer.
J. Bernstein, 1987, "The life it brings—I," *The New Yorker,* January 26, 1987, 35.

Page 119:
Playfulness and creativity.
J. Dansky and I. Silverman, 1973, "Effects of play on associative fluency in preschool-aged children," *Developmental Psychology 9,* 38–43.

Page 119:
Children's fantasy play.
M. W. Watson and C. J. Boyatzis, 1987, "An assessment of fantasy in the play of preschool children" (Unpublished manuscript, Brandeis University, Waltham, MA).

Page 120:
California study of creative children's homes.
D. M. Harrington, J. H. Block, and J. Block, 1987, "Testing aspects of Carl Rogers's theory of creative environments: Child-rearing antecedents of creative potential in young adolescents," *Journal of Personality and Social Psychology 52,* 851–56.

Page 123:
Father absence and creativity.
R. S. Albert, 1980, "Family positions and the attainment of eminence: A study of special family experiences," *Gifted Child Quarterly 24,* 87–95.

Page 123:
Childhood traumas and creativity.
J. S. Dacey, 1987, "Discriminating characteristics of the families of highly creative adolescents" (Unpublished manuscript, Center for Research on Creativity, Lexington, MA).

Chapter 7

Page 130:
Study of controlling and noncontrolling instructions.
W. S. Grolnick and R. M. Ryan, 1987, "Autonomy in children's learning: An experimental and individual difference investigation," *Journal of Personality and Social Psychology 52,* 890–98.

Page 131:
Autonomy questionnaire study.
E. L. Deci et al., 1981, "An instrument to assess adults' orientations toward control versus autonomy with children: Reflections on intrinsic motivation and perceived competence," *Journal of Educational Psychology 52,* 233–48.

Page 133:
Research on open versus traditional classrooms.
R. A. Horowitz, 1979, "Psychological effects of the open classroom," *Review of Educational Research 49,* 71–85.

Pages 149–150:
Quote from demonstration with gifted children.
S. Wasserman, 1982, "The gifted can't weigh that giraffe," *Phi Delta Kappan 63,* 621.

Page 150:
The Performance Syndrome.
C. S. Dweck, 1986, "Motivational processes affecting learning," *American Psychologist 41,* 1040–48.

Page 153:
Study on training intrinsic motivation.
T. M. Amabile, B. A. Hennessey, and M. Martirage (in press) "Immunizing children against the negative effects of reward," *Contemporary Education Psychology.*

Chapter 8

Page 169:

The jigsaw technique.
E. Aronson et al., 1978, *The jigsaw classroom* (Beverly Hills, CA: Sage Publications).

ACKNOWLEDGMENTS

Grateful acknowledgment is hereby given to the following sources for permissions to reprint from the material listed below:

Tables from "Testing Aspects of Carl Roger's Theory of Creative Environments: Child-rearing Antecedents of Creative Potential in Your Adolescents" by D. M. Harrington, J. H. Block, and J. Block in *Journal of Personality and Social Psychology, 52,* (1987). Copyright © 1987 by the American Psychological Association. Used by permission of the authors and publisher.

"Feyneman and the Visualization of Space-Time Processes" by S. S. Schweber in *Review of Modern Physics, 58* (1986). Used by permission of the author.

Excerpts from *Albert Einstein* by Banesh Hoffman, copyright © 1972 by Helen Dukas and Banesh Hoffman. Used by permission of Viking Penguin, Inc.

Letter by Robert Oppenheimer to Frank Oppenheimer from *The Life It Brings* by Jeremy Bernstein, copyright © 1987 by Jeremy Bernstein. This material was originally published in slightly different form in *The New Yorker,* January 26, 1987. Used by permission of Houghton Mifflin Company.

Excerpts from *Blackberry Winter: My Earlier Years* by Margaret Mead, copyright © 1972 by Margaret Mead. Used by permission of William Morrow and Company, Inc.

Excerpts from "Present at the Creation" by F. A. Bernstein first appeared in *People,* May 5, 1986, pp. 95–99. Used by permission of the author.

Quote by Eudora Welty in an article by Jean Stafford was first published by *The Boston Globe,* October 2, 1986. Used by permission of *The Boston Globe.*

Quote by Arthur Schawlow in an article titled "Going for the Gaps" was first published in *The Stanford Magazine,* Fall 1982. Used by permission.

Excerpts from the autobiography of Albert Einstein in *Albert Einstein: Philosopher-scientist* by P. Schilpp. Used by permission of Library of Living Philosophers.

Excerpts from *Ansel Adams: An Autobiography* by Ansel Adams with Mary Street Alinder, copyright © 1985 by The Trustees of the Ansel Adams Publishing Trust. Used by permission of Little, Brown and Company, Inc.

Excerpts from *Joys and Sorrows: Reflections by Pablo Casals,* copyright © 1970 by Albert E. Kahn. Used by permission of Simon & Schuster, Inc.

Excerpt from *The Journals of Sylvia Plath* edited by T. Hughes and F. McCullough. Used by permission of Doubleday, a division of the Bantam Doubleday Dell Publishing Group, Inc.

Excerpt from "The Gifted Can't Weigh That Giraffe" by S. Wasserman first appeared in *Phi Delta Kappan, 63* (1982). Used by permission of the author.

Excerpt from *Les Nourritures Terrestres* by André Gide, copyright © Editions Gallimard 1917. Used by permission of the publisher.

Excerpt from "Why We Must Continue to Be Explorers" by Carl Sagan, copyright © 1987 by Carl Sagan, first appeared in *Parade Magazine.* Used by permission of the author.

Excerpt from *And So It Goes: Adventures in Television* by Linda Ellerbee, copyright © 1986 by Linda Ellerbee. Used by permission of The Putnam Publishing Group.

Excerpt from *Mozart: His Life and Times* by Peggy Woodford from *The Illustrated Lives of the Great Composers* series. Used by permission of Omnibus Press.

Excerpts from "Precocious Child on a Mission" by J. Logan first appeared in *The Boston Globe,* February 8, 1987. Used by permission of *The Boston Globe.*

Excerpt from "Rapt by the Radio" by John Updike first appeared in *The Boston Globe, Literati on the Red Sox,* October 6, 1986. Used by permission of Random House, Inc.

Excerpts from "Eliot and Friends" by Eileen Simpson first appeared in *The New York Times.*

Quote by Dostoevsky from *Writers on Writing* by W. Allen. Published in London by Phoenix House, 1948.

INDEX